BEYOND PERSUASION

Communication Strategies for Healthcare Managers in the Digital Age

Second Edition

The advent of social media has forever changed how organizations communicate with the public, and healthcare organizations are no exception. *Beyond Persuasion* provides healthcare managers with a guide to using strategic communication to meet both personal and professional objectives in the digital age.

Whether healthcare managers are conducting meetings with employees, answering massive amounts of email, or keeping up with Twitter feeds, their success ultimately depends on their strategic communication skills. The first book to offer a strategic approach to managerial communication in health care, *Beyond Persuasion* is full of valuable information on issues such as how to develop fundamental skills, communicate strategically with internal groups such as employees and medical staff, and develop relationships with the external community and both traditional and new media.

In this new edition, Patricia J. Parsons has added new references and resources and has updated the text with fresh material on how to weave social media tools, tactics, strategies, and policies into the fundamental discussion about communication as a personal, professional, and organizational priority.

PATRICIA J. PARSONS is Professor of Communication Studies at Mount Saint Vincent University in Halifax.

Beyond Persuasion

Communication Strategies for Healthcare Managers in the Digital Age

Second Edition

PATRICIA J. PARSONS

UNIVERSITY OF TORONTO PRESS
Toronto Buffalo London

ISBN 978-1-4426-4721-3 (cloth)
ISBN 978-1-4426-1534-2 (paper)

Printed on acid-free, 100% post-consumer recycled paper with
vegetable-based inks.

Publication cataloguing information is available from Library and Archives
Canada

University of Toronto Press acknowledges the financial assistance to its
publishing program of the Canada Council for the Arts and the Ontario
Arts Council.

 Canada Council   Conseil des Arts
for the Arts   du Canada

University of Toronto Press acknowledges the financial support of the
Government of Canada through the Canada Book Fund for its publishing
activities.

Contents

Level IV: Crises and Issues

Preface

There are four ways, and only four ways, in which we have contact with the world. We are evaluated and classified by these four contacts: what we do, how we look, what we say, and how we say it.

– Dale Carnegie

When I first began thinking about how to teach about strategic communication for healthcare managers, it occurred to me that much could be learned from a framework that emulated a computer-based, role-playing game.

Many years ago, I watched my young son manoeuvre his way through a maze of obstacles and tasks, strategically figuring out the best way to achieve mastery of the challenges so that he could move to a higher level of performance. As I thumbed through the pages of the strategy guide, I began to see a connection between the strategic achievement of levels in this game of medieval knights and battles, and the everyday strategies, tools, and tactics that are so necessary to healthcare organizations seeking to nurture their relationships with important constituencies.

I was intrigued by this comparison because it occurred to me that with communication in the context of healthcare management – one of my personal and professional passions – there are "levels" through which the most skilled executive communicators must progress.

Just as in a computer game, learning how to manoeuvre your executive team successfully through a lower level provides you with considerable skill and knowledge to achieve your objectives when the situation is more complicated. The difference between the game and the reality, however, lies in the fact that in our real-life situations, a higher-level obstacle can pop up even before we're really ready. And although many managers consider communication to be a tool to achieve consensus (in other words, to persuade others to their way of thinking!), healthcare communication goes way beyond persuasion.

Traditionally, communication for healthcare managers has focused almost exclusively on the technical and interpersonal level of communication skills. I submit that a clear-eyed focus on the more complex levels of communication – strategic communication – is long overdue.

I believe that my conclusion is supported by others:

Providers who are poor communicators are sued most often.[1]

A solid HCMN [healthcare management] curriculum integrates the liberal arts general education requirements of communication (written and oral)[2] with other skills required of managers …

The next generation of [healthcare] managers should have effective communication skills (written and verbal) …[3]

… and perhaps the most important observation of all …

Very few advanced degree programs in health administration and medicine focus on teaching effective communication skills.[4]

These observations coupled with the fact that basic textbooks on managerial skill building for healthcare management students usually devote fewer than ten pages to communication skills suggests that there is much still to be done in helping healthcare managers improve their knowledge and skills in the area of strategic communication.

Indeed, in the list of skills and/or knowledge that are being sought by employers in many business areas, including health care, communication skills – both written and verbal – are listed either number one or, less often, number two. In spite of the fact that communication skills are so highly valued, many healthcare managers still need help. Jamie Haeuser, chief operating officer of Woman's Hospital in Baton Rouge (LA); and Paul Preston, a professor of management at the University of Montevallo (AL) (who is also the leader of the "Sharpening Executive Skills" seminar[5]) have said the following:

Effective communications don't just happen – they are the product of a sustained and focused effort to sharpen skills and hone abilities.

Healthcare executives are wise to go beyond "common sense" in applying proven communication techniques to their most important challenges. The result will be improved performance and more effective relationships.[6]

It seems clear that more resources are needed for both neophyte healthcare managers as well as their more experienced counterparts to assist them to develop those coveted communication skills.

When an earlier incarnation of this book was published way back in 2001, the communication landscape was vastly different. We had no idea of the extent to which digital media, new media, social media or whatever you might call it, would change public communication (and no less so personal communication) forever. The original purpose of *Beyond Persuasion* was to provide the readers with the knowledge, attitudes, and skills to use communication strategies and tactics to manage their organizations' and their own relationships with important constituencies. Academic programs in health administration were sadly lacking in coursework on strategic communication at both the undergraduate and the graduate levels, and that has not changed. Many healthcare administrators are still unaware that they lack these important skills, the lack of which is magnified by the communication changes of the digital age. It would be something of an understatement to say that much in the world of communication – and health care – has changed since then.

Over the past dozen years as we have moved into the new millennium and have seen the penetration of the digital approach to communication, I've made the following observations that lead me to believe that this information ought to be collected, added to basic strategic communication considerations, and become the book you now see.

• The landscape of public communication has changed dramatically and forever. Anyone who works in any public communication area (media, corporate communication, advertising, social marketing, health promotion, to name a few) recognizes that the advent of social media and its uptake by the populace has changed forever how organizations, including healthcare organizations, communicate and develop relationships with their important publics. The concept of "controlling the message" to achieve specific objectives seems as antiquated as a dial telephone. The participatory nature of the new social media means that even in situations like crises, the message is out before anyone in the affected organization has time to contemplate the "message." We learned this very quickly in the wake of the Virginia Tech shootings in 2007, and crisis communication has never been the same.

- Healthcare managers are becoming more interested in communication insofar as they want material about social media. In February 2008, I was asked by the American College of Healthcare Executives (Chicago) to conduct a webinar on social media for healthcare managers all over the continent. Most had very little knowledge about these new ways of communicating, but the participants recognized that they needed to know about this – whether they like it or not. Since that time I've been teaching social media courses at both the undergraduate and graduate level to students in corporate and science communication.
- Healthcare managers and educators are beginning to recognize the importance of certain specific communication skills as evidenced by the number of courses that now have writing and other communication components included.
- Mass media (both traditional and new) have increasing influence on healthcare decisions that are made by the general populace. Managerial decisions of necessity are often made based on reactions to what's in the headlines since that's what the populace comes to believe no matter how much misinformation may be in evidence.
- Basic communication skills, such as writing, making presentations, and knowing how to give an interview are even more important in the age of blogging and micro blogging, organizational podcasting, online video sharing, and internal social networking to name a few.
- There is an increasing need for materials for educators to use to help neophyte healthcare managers develop these skills.

In this book I hope you'll find a way to weave social media tools, tactics, strategies, and policies into the fundamental discussion about communication as a personal, professional, and organizational priority.

Dale Carnegie's admonition about the "only four ways" by which we are classified and evaluated by the world apply equally to healthcare organizations as well. In fact, organizational actions, as communicated through both behaviour and words, become their public image or "look." And even neophyte public relations practitioners know that *perception is reality*. What people *believe* to be true is true for them in all its consequences, and they will act according to those beliefs. It is your job as a healthcare manager to ensure that what they believe about your organization is congruent with what you perceive is reality. Strategic communication through word and action is the way to accomplish this.

The bottom line is that strategic communication skills at the interpersonal, group, and organizational levels are crucially important for healthcare managers in today's world of communication overload. Whether conducting a meeting with employees, answering ever-increasing email, or fielding reporters' questions at a media conference, both your own personal skills and how you use them in the overall strategic communication plan for your organization are important to your personal success, as well as to the success of your organization in achieving its mission.

Over the years I have observed that graduate programs in health administration are sadly lacking in course work on strategic communication as a management tool. Consequently, neophyte healthcare executives often find themselves lacking fundamental concepts in how to best cultivate and use relationships with a variety of audiences, including the media. Indeed, healthcare executives whose educational background may be in business administration are essentially in the same situation. In any case, application of strategic communication concepts and practices is fundamentally an on-the-job problem.

How to Use This Book

I have divided the material in this book into four levels, on the premise that the ideas in Level I are fundamental to those in Level II, and on up. Theoretically, mastery of the ideas, skills, tools, and tactics in one level should assist you in successfully achieving mastery at a higher level. However, as I mentioned earlier, challenges of a somewhat higher order often can and do emerge before you are really ready. Thus, the material in this book isn't entirely linear. Figure i.i illustrates what I mean about building strong foundations. (It might remind you a bit of first-year psychology and Abraham Maslow's Hierarchy of Needs.)

Level I provides an overview of professional foundations of communication in healthcare management as well as a detailed examination of the personal foundations needed – that is, your skills. This will allow you to consider and assess your own communication skills on a number of levels including both oral and written. Level II suggests that achieving communication goals begins close to home and that, in fact, neglect of this level leads to more problems at the following

Figure i.i Levels of Complexity in the Development of Strategic
Communication Skills

Level IV: Issues crises and
social responsibility

Level III: Communication
with external audiences

Level II: Communication
with internal audiences

Level I: Foundations:
Personal/professional

levels. Level III examines external communication, which is important
in healthcare management. However, this discussion is not meant to
be an exhaustive examination of all the external constituencies health-
related organizations need to concern themselves with (for that kind
of a discussion, you will need to consult a textbook about public relations). Finally, Level IV broadens its view to examine crisis communication and the issue of social responsibility in healthcare communication.

Along the way, you will have an opportunity to figure out how you
stack up in both your attitudes and your communication skills. In addition, at the end of each chapter you will find some guidance on where
to look for further information.

Patricia J. Parsons
2013

BEYOND PERSUASION

Communication Strategies for Healthcare
Managers in the Digital Age

Second Edition

LEVEL I

Personal and Professional Foundations

The following six chapters introduce you to a variety of fundamental characteristics of healthcare communication in both the broad professional and the narrower personal contexts. The broad issues provide you, as an individual manager, with a working framework that we will use as our shared understanding and vocabulary to describe the concepts.

This section also allows you to take a very detailed look at your own communication skills. Together we will explore your attitudes and skills in interpersonal, written, and oral communications and explore your use of new media.

These concepts require personal commitment and mastery for full achievement of communication objectives as a manager and for your organization.

1 Communication: A Management Tool

To the man who has only a hammer in his tool kit, every problem looks like a nail.

– Abraham Maslow

Let's begin by looking in on a day in the hypothetical life of one health-care manager.

By the time Michael Smith had a moment to even look at his watch it was 9:20 a.m. Already this morning he had met with his senior managers about a pending labour dispute with their technical staff, and he had sifted through sixty-four e-mail messages. He had answered the most urgent of them; taken a quick look at two departmental budgets; fielded a call from an irate board member whose daughter had not gotten the job she wanted on his staff; and now his secretary had just buzzed him to say that Carla MacDonald, his PR director, was waiting anxiously to see him. And he hadn't even had his coffee yet. Such is the life of a hospital CEO, he thought wryly.

Michael had been the CEO of St Swithin's Health Sciences Center for almost five years, and he actually liked his job despite the fact that there were days like these when there seemed to be one problem after another; he knew that Carla needed to discuss one of the most pressing with him. St Swithin's was caught between one of their most prestigious research scientists and a pharmaceutical company. The researcher had discovered that a drug she was testing on a group of patients did what the manufacturer said it would, but she had also found that it had significant, deleterious – indeed life-threatening – side effects. As a result, she had discontinued using it and then gone public with her findings so that other researchers using the drug experimentally could protect their patients, too, in spite of an apparent gag order by the drug company. The drug company was preparing to sue the doctor and St Swithin's for breaching a confidentiality clause in the research grant contract. To make matters worse, the researcher and many of the other doctors at St Swithin's were now accusing the hospital of not standing behind its researchers and the ethical protection of patients. They were accusing hospital administration of bowing to the pressures of big business.

"Michael," Carla began, taking a seat in front of his desk and opening a large file folder full of papers. "We need to plan a media conference."

"Why can't we just send out releases? You know how much I hate facing the press."

Carla was adamant that they couldn't deal with all the hospital's relationship issues by sending out media releases and newsletters. Michael could write a dynamite memo or letter or e-mail message, and that was how he preferred to communicate. In fact, he was one of the few people he knew who had welcomed electronic communication with open arms – no longer would he be required to have small talk with anyone. To him it was a miracle. Carla, however, did not share his view.

On his desk she placed five pages of media printouts from the Internet. There were bona fide news stories, blog posts, Facebook updates, and a plethora of tweets. He had already seen the news stories. He sighed and knew that he was going to have to listen to her.

Put yourself in Michael Smith's chair for a moment, and consider how you would feel about his issues.

Abraham Maslow was the psychology luminary who pioneered the idea that people who are hungry, cold, or in physical pain are not likely to be interested in reaching for self-actualization. His work in understanding human behaviour also indicated that people need a wide variety of skills to deal with the equally wide variety of challenges that come their way through life. Managers in healthcare facilities and organizations face ever more diverse issues on a daily basis, and their skill sets need to be eclectic as well.

Communication issues and the relationship problems and opportunities that arise from these issues require managers with a high level of knowledge about modern communication, an attitude that allows them to apply that knowledge in a strategic way, and highly developed personal skills that can be applied in diverse situations. The bottom line is that you need a variety of tools in your management tool kit, and communication skills are an important key to the successful application of most other tools and techniques of management.

The Manager as Communicator

In 1955, the *Harvard Business Review* published a now-classic article (which they republished in 1974) that posed and answered the following question: *What observable skills does an effective executive demonstrate?* The author divided the skills into technical, human, and conceptual, and indicated that the executive must be "skillful in communicating to others, in their own contexts, what he [sic] means by his [sic] behavior."[1]

Recent literature continues to support this view, yet managers of all stripes still seem to be unprepared in the area of personal communication skills. Conrad and Newberry (2012) concluded that "… the literature supports the lack of preparedness of new graduates with respect to business communication skills despite a consensus among practitioners and academia of those skills sets' importance …"[2] Their study suggests that there continues to be an argument between those who hold that face-to-face skills are paramount, whereas others consider that in these days of growing electronic communication, skills in written communication are the top priority. Regardless of the order of priority, if we examine a healthcare manager's various functions and roles, we can develop a clear picture of where communication skills are key.

Defining Management Yet Again

Regardless of when you first study management and at what level – undergraduate or graduate – the term *management* as a construct is a bit like the word *personality*. Psychologists have difficulty defining it; there seem to be as many definitions as there are psychologists studying it. The same is true of the term *management*. Most definitions, however, have some distinct commonalities.

First, management is a process of getting things done efficiently and effectively. It is not something that exists only at one point in time, but is continuous and dynamic, and in the process of "getting things done," specific outcomes can be measured.

Second, management accomplishes its goals through people as well as through the strategic use of other organizational resources, including time and money. What's crucial here is that people are the key to a manager's ability to get things done.

Finally, most authors of basic texts in management agree that managers use four fundamental activities to accomplish their goals: planning, organizing, leading, and controlling.[3]

Let's take a closer look at where communication plays a role in these aspects of management.

Interpersonal skills and roles

If part of what a manager does is accomplish goals with and through people, little doubt exists that a manager must be a master communicator, first on an interpersonal level. Most people think they know what it means to have good interpersonal skills. They believe that an individual who appears to get along well with co-workers possesses these good skills. This is, however, an oversimplification when we're talking about a healthcare manager's skill set. A manager with good interpersonal skills is able to assess the situation in which the person-to-person interaction is taking place, understand the communication skill level of the other person, communicate his or her message clearly, listen well, and respond appropriately.

It is also true that managers play a variety of interpersonal roles, which might be traditionally described as the figurehead role, the leadership role, and the liaison role.[4]

- As a *figurehead*, the healthcare manager might speak at a meeting or conference of healthcare administration students, or hand out diplomas at the graduation ceremonies of the medical technology course hosted by his or her hospital.
- In a *leadership* role, the manager is the one with the vision for the future of the organization, but also the responsibility to communicate that vision to the employees to ensure their buy-in and support for its accomplishment. This role requires high-level interpersonal communication skills, as well as proficiency in the use of mediated communication (which will be discussed later).
- The *liaison* role is played almost daily by managers at all levels within healthcare organizations. Henry Mintzberg, author of the now-classic text *The Nature of Managerial Work*, sees this liaison role

as one of gathering information from sources external to the manager's own work unit.[5] When the vice president of administrative services has a meeting with the transplant coordinators to gather information about how they are setting up flights to receive outside organ procurement teams, he or she is functioning in an internal liaison role. When the director of the transplant program meets with other such directors from other hospitals, this is an external liaison role. When the CEO meets with government representatives to discuss Medicare, this is also an external liaison.

Central to the success of each of these encounters is the individual manager's communication skills at the interpersonal level. Interpersonal skills are important, but they aren't the only kind of communication skills that are crucial to the healthcare manager's success.

Proximity

It might be a good time to consider the current issue of proximity when we examine interpersonal skills. Is it necessary to be in the same room with someone to use your interpersonal skills?

Not necessarily. Today's technological work environment often requires us to use mediated communication rather than direct, person-to-person communication. First, consider the telephone. You are not actually in the same room with the person with whom you are talking, and thus the communication values of such things as nonverbal cues are not available to you in interpreting what is being said or in conveying your own message. Your ability to communicate with that person on an interpersonal level, however, is still very important – it is just a bit different than if you were in the same room.

What about voice mail? E-mail? Although good interpersonal skills might improve your ability to use these to their best advantage, they do require somewhat different proficiencies. And although making a presentation at a large staff meeting might seem like an interpersonal approach, in fact it, too, requires a different set of skills again.

Here are some examples of where interpersonal skills are important in healthcare management:

- daily interaction with close staff
- interaction with medical staff
- interaction with individual board members

- negotiating with labour organizations
- interviewing staff and others (in the same room or over the Internet via webcam)
- disciplining staff
- being interviewed by media
- talking to patients and their families
- telephone calls
- internal or external meetings

Written Communication

Healthcare managers also require a high level of achievement in the area of written communication. If we examine the managerial activities already mentioned (planning, organizing, leading, and controlling) it becomes clear that many of these require written communication for their successful accomplishment.

William Zinsser is arguably one of America's finest writing teachers. In his now-classic book *On Writing Well* (originally published in 1976) he lays it on the line by telling the reader this: "Few people realize how badly they write."[6] You may have graduated with a master's degree in health or business administration and written dozens of papers, perhaps even a thesis. You have written more exams than you care to remember and taken hundreds of pages of notes, but can you truly say that all of this makes you a good writer? If you didn't study applied communications at the college or university level, then it is likely that no one ever really taught you to write or evaluated your writing as a key part of the process. Writing, however, is fundamental to almost every other type of communication that is important in health care (or any other industry for that matter). Indeed, the roles and activities of managers, by their very nature, require excellence in written communication.

Here are some examples of where written communication skills are important in healthcare management:

- everyday e-mail
- letters to both internal and external individuals and groups
- correspondence with government
- speeches and presentations to employees, community groups, or government

- preparation for media interviews
- editing the written work of lower-level staff
- your submission to the newsletter or annual report
- reports and proposals
- your submission to the hospital blog
- writing proposals

Many basic textbooks on communicating within organizations seem to give short shrift to important aspects of written communication. Perhaps this is the reason why so many managers enter their positions believing that writing is something that they have already learned by osmosis. Whereas writing requires a good grasp of the fundamentals of our language (spelling, punctuation, grammar, and syntax), it demands even more. Healthcare managers must be able to mould their writing to achieve specific and often diverse results, and must be able to target their writing to a variety of audiences including medical and nonmedical staff, patients and their families, community groups, government, and the media. Writing academic papers in college is not necessarily good preparation for these challenges.

Presentation Skills

The final skill set that is an important key to success in healthcare communication is presentation skills. This does not refer to chairing meetings, rather to situations where you find yourself having to make an appearance before a group and must be prepared to say something that is meaningful and targeted to that specific audience. Sometimes the group is interested in what you have to say – and sometimes it emphatically is not. Regardless of the reception, you have to be prepared and effective in front of your audience.

An oft-cited statistic claims that when people are polled about what they are most afraid of, public speaking ranks ahead of snakes, spiders, and even death. Whether or not this is actually true, it is likely that at least some healthcare managers are uncomfortable making presentations, and may even try to avoid every such situation. Arguably, it is impossible to be a truly effective healthcare manager without highly developed presentation skills. Perhaps one of the most compelling reasons that some individuals fear public speaking is that their skill set is not at the level it should be.

Here are some examples of where presentation skills are important in healthcare management:

- facing the media at a press conference
- presenting the annual report to the board
- speaking to community groups
- acting as master of ceremonies at social functions
- conducting workshops for peers at conferences
- pitching to government or private groups for project support

Clearly communication skills are an important key to success as a healthcare manager. Now is a good time to figure out what we really mean by the term *communication*.

Communication in Theory and Practice

Just as the term *management* was difficult to define precisely, so too is the term *communication*. In fact, the author of one classic book on communication theory lists 126 such attempts![7] Some of the definitions refer specifically to verbal communication, while others are broader. Some focus on the goals of communication while others focus on the medium. Although all of this is useful for a prolonged discussion of the semantics of the issue, we need a clear definition of healthcare communication upon which we can all agree. For the purposes of this book, we will define it as follows:

Healthcare communication is a two-way process of informing, persuading, and sharing ideas while utilizing the most appropriate medium for the situation and for the participants.

It is crucially important to recognize that although the purpose of much of your communication activity on a daily basis might appear to be one-way (e-mail, letters, and meetings), the reality is that there needs to be an opportunity for a two-way process within every communication encounter. The reason for this is that communication is the foundation upon which relationships are built (more about this in the next section). Even a small e-mail message designed to provide the receivers with specific information needs to be open to feedback.

The simplest model of communication in health care is illustrated in Figure 1.1.

Figure 1.1 The Simplest Model of Communication

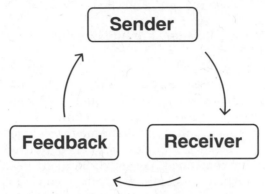

In one scenario, the healthcare manager is the sender of the message, the receiver picks up that message, and a feedback loop allows the manager to know of the receiver's response. Did the receiver actually receive the message? Did the receiver understand the message? Does the receiver have anything to add to the message? Does the receiver agree/disagree with the message? The answers to all of these questions are useful information for the manager. The manager who ignores this aspect of the communication process does so at his or her peril! More recently, with the advent of social media, the receiver providing feedback is just as likely to be a member of one of the organization's external publics. The loop, however, is the same in both cases.

This simple model, however, tells only part of the story. Twenty-first-century communication is focused not only on that feedback loop and responding to it, but on *engagement*. A simple dialogue is no longer enough. There is much more of an emphasis on finding ways to facilitate behaviours that are supportive of an organization's objectives and that involve active participation of the target publics. Only when the communication targets become an active participant are they truly engaged with the organization – a situation that supports strong relationships. The social media tools of the digital age have made this engagement both important and unavoidable.

Finally in terms of communication models, it's important to note that although two-way communication and engagement seem desirable, they may not be appropriate in all situations. Making that decision is part of the strategic planning process, and integration of communication planning in the development of operational strategy is the whole point of expanding the view of what communication can and cannot accomplish for you and your organization.

Communication and Relationship Building

If we look more critically at the simple communication model above, we find that it doesn't really provide any indication of *why* we might communicate. Initially, we might consider that communication is required *to inform and to persuade*. If we examine this more closely, it is clear that communication theorists aren't too far off base when they tell us that we communicate to fulfil a human need. (Indeed, a number of telecommunication companies have based their advertising campaigns on this concept.) Whereas all of this is useful when we are talking about communication within our own personal worlds, are the same reasons sufficient to support the need to be a highly skilled communicator in your job in health care? Not really.

In the context of your job as a healthcare manager, one of the most important reasons to consider the quality of your communication is because the relationships that you have with other individuals – and that your organization has with other groups and organizations – often originate directly from the quality of the communication that has flowed between you and these others.

If we go back to the scenario played out at the beginning of this chapter, we find our hypothetical healthcare manager Michael Smith in a situation that has implications for his own and his hospital's relationships with a variety of individuals and groups. If Michael is a master communicator and has placed a high value on his communication over the past four years, it will be much easier for him to deal with the current situation.

- If Michael has cultivated a good interpersonal relationship with the medical director, that individual will feel comfortable going directly to Michael to discuss the current situation with the researcher. It is then less likely that the medical staff members who are concerned about the hospital's commitment to, and support of, their research will discuss the situation with the media before administration knows about it.
- If Michael has been strategic about his communication efforts with the medical staff as a group, the positive relationship would make it less likely for them to jump to conclusions about how senior administration is handling this situation.

- If Michael has always been strategic about his communication with his hospital board, and he has maintained a policy of keeping them informed, there is less likelihood that any board members will feel that they have to enter into the fray without first allowing senior administration to have their say.
- If Michael has been an effective, credible spokesperson when members of the media have asked to interview him from time to time over the years, they are more likely to provide his hospital's senior administration with a fair hearing and airing in the media.
- If Michael has been a solid member of the community, supporting community issues and events, providing his leadership and expertise when necessary – developed a good relationship – they will cut him a bit of slack before forming their own opinions of the hospital's behaviour.

These are just a few of the crucial long-term relationships that can have either a positive or negative effect on both the day-to-day activities of a healthcare organization and on crisis situations. While it may seem at first glance that it is the organization's relationship, rather than the manager's, with these groups that is most crucial, the CEO's own personal communication skills and knowledge will play a key part. At lower levels in the organizational hierarchy, the situation for managers is similar. In this particular situation, the director of pharmaceutical services may find him or herself on the firing line. This individual's strategic communication skills will also play a role in the direction of the outcome, positive or negative.

Public Relations

Before we go any further, we need to understand another term and another role within your organization. That is the public relations (PR) function in health care, and how your own mastery of strategic communication plays a role in that managerial area.

Public relations uses communications tools and techniques to help organizations develop and maintain relationships.[8] What this means to you is that your public relations department should be expected to have expertise in all areas of strategic communication for the purposes of assisting your organization to achieve the goodwill of important publics both internally and externally. Recent analyses of the aftermath of crises has taught us that it is important to establish what might be referred to as a "reservoir of good will" in advance of the requirement for it.[9]

In addition, you should be able to rely on them for expert advice in the development of your own skills, whether you are the CEO or a manager at a lower level. If, however, you are a manager in a small organization that does not have a PR staff, then you probably have an even more crucially important role in strategic communications. (We will go into more detail about this in chapter 9.)

The bottom line is that in your role as a manager in a healthcare facility or other health-related organization, every communication encounter that you personally have with any person or group inside or outside your working environment will have an effect on both yours and the organization's relationship with a variety of constituencies. And the goodwill of these groups could be key to the accomplishment of your mission.

Targets for Healthcare Communication

Healthcare managers communicate with a wide variety of people and groups on a daily basis. Some of these encounters are planned, while others simply spring up during the course of the day's work. If you were to make a list of the number of communication encounters you have in the run of a working day, how many could you come up with?

Here are the important groups with whom you communicate. Most of the people and groups on your own list should fit into one of the following general classifications:

- employees
- medical staff
- board members
- financial donors/potential financial donors
- patients and their families
- future patients and their families
- community members
- financial institutions
- government
- the media
- community health-related organizations
- regulatory bodies
- professional organizations
- suppliers
- union leadership

You probably noted already that these broad groupings could be broken down even more finely, but for now this general list allows us to consider the implications of the encounters.

Each of these groups has a different reason for wanting to communicate with you, and you have a different objective for every communication encounter you initiate. We do, however, need to note right from the start of any discussion of targeted, goal-driven communication, that the advent of social media has forever changed the public communication landscape. All of our stakeholders now have access to forms of mass media and audiences that were unheard of in years gone by. Indeed, gone are the days of controlling the message to the extent we might like. That said, honing your own skills can put you in a much stronger position when you are the receiver of the communication.

The question is this: are you ready to communicate effectively with each of these groups to achieve important strategic objectives for yourself and your organization? By the end of the next few chapters, you should be ready to answer that question more accurately.

Chapter 1 Key Points

1. Communication is a crucial leadership tool for success in healthcare management.
2. Communication skills at the interpersonal level are important in managerial roles, including the leadership role, the figure-head role, and the liaison role.
3. Written communication skills are fundamental to almost all aspects of healthcare management, including strategic planning, relationship building, and organizational development.
4. Highly developed presentation skills are often the key difference between the manager and the leader.
5. Whereas two-way communication and audience engagement are desirable, some situations may require one-way strategic control.
6. An understanding of the public relations function in health care provides the manager with a broader basis for being strategic in his or her communication encounters.

For Your Bookshelf

Clampitt, Phillip. *Communicating for Managerial Effectiveness*. Thousand Oaks, CA: Sage, 2010.

Hynes, Gerald. *Managerial Communication: Strategies and Applications*. New York: McGraw-Hill/Irwin, 2010.

Parsons, Patricia J. *A Manager's Guide to P.R. Projects: A Practical Approach*. Mahwah, NJ: Lawrence Erlbaum, 2003.

On the Web

Management Skills List. http://www.buzzle.com/articles/management-skills list.html

Management Styles. http://www.rpi.edu/dept/advising/free_enterprise/business_structures/management_styles.htm

Management versus Leadership. http://managementhelp.org/ldrship/ldrship.htm#anchor2078406

2 The Strategic Communication Process

The plan is nothing. Planning is everything!

– Dwight D. Eisenhower

Any manager worth his or her salt already knows a great deal about being strategic. However, as healthcare management consultant Alan Zuckerman points out, "Failure to *implement* a strategic plan is one of the most common flaws of the strategic planning process" (emphasis added).[1]

When it comes to communication by healthcare managers, not only is the plan not implemented, but it is often neglected entirely. For many managers, communication is simply something that they do every day, giving it little thought and even less strategic consideration. Before we move into our discussion of communication as a strategic process, let's look in on Michael Smith, our hospital CEO and his PR director.

"Okay, Carla," Michael said, reading one of the computer printouts in front of him on his desk. "We'll have a press conference."

"It isn't quite that simple," Carla said as she gathered the papers and slipped them into her portfolio.

Michael sighed. Nothing ever was.

"Everything we say to the media has implications for a lot of other people and groups."

"I suppose you mean the medical staff?" Michael said.

"That's only the beginning." Carla pulled another sheaf of papers out and began to lay them on the desk. There were figures with circles and arrows, charts, tables, and pages of narrative.

Step by step, Carla took Michael through her thoughts about what she called a domino effect. She explained to him that whatever he and the rest of the hospital said to anyone about the problem with the pharmaceutical company would have an effect on any number of other individuals and groups. She explained that there might even be groups that hadn't formed yet or that they hadn't thought about yet.

For example, in their midst they had nurse – researchers from the university whose response would have to be considered. All employees would be concerned if they thought that the hospital wouldn't even stand behind their high-profile, apparently highly prized researchers. Where would that leave them? Then, of course, there were the citizen groups who were concerned with the safety of clinical trials of new drugs.

The bottom line was that before they did anything, they would have to know the answers to a number of key questions:

- What were they doing about the situation?
- What were they prepared to say?
- How would they say it?
- To whom would they say it, and how would the message have to be tailored to the interests and concerns of each group?
- What method would they use to get the message to the important groups?
- Who would be the messenger for each group?
- When would each of the groups receive their message?
- How would they know that the message was received accurately?
- How would they gauge the overall response to their approach?

Carla and Michael together determined that above all they needed to safeguard the good reputation of their hospital, but that their own mission and philosophy determined that they had to be as honest as they could with their important constituencies without jeopardizing anyone's right to privacy. That included the privacy of both patients and staff members. With the answers to these questions and a values-based framework, they were on solid ground to move forward to accomplish their goal.

"We need a plan!" How often have you heard someone say this, or even said it yourself? Webster's dictionary defines a *plan* as "an arrangement of means or steps for the attainment of some object; a scheme; method; design ... a model of action."[2] So, what you are really saying is that you need an intention to do something. Having a plan is a good thing, but simply having a plan does not by its mere existence mean that anything will be done with it. Whereas planning as an exercise may be important, the process of implementation in healthcare communication planning is key. Thus, we need to consider communication planning as a process, a term that is defined more as a "forward movement."[3] This concept of movement is crucial.

Seat-of-the-Pants Communications

"We better call in PR!" When do you usually hear this cry for help? Before a problem has occurred? Or does it seem more common that this phrase is heard when a problem has arisen and some relationship needs patching?

For too many years, healthcare organizations took many of their important relationships that were built on communication processes for granted. Thus, communication became more of a fire-fighting, rather than a fire-preventing process. This fire-fighting paradigm is illustrated by the following:

- We won't bother to develop a dialogue with our nursing staff until they threaten to go on strike.
- We don't need to initiate contact with the government until they threaten our Medicare payments.
- I don't need to give any thought to how I answer my e-mail–until someone feels he or she has been slighted.

Many problems that organizations face with their relationships are a direct result of dealing with communication issues in a reactive, rather than a proactive, way.

Strategic Steps and the Domino Effect

To take a proactive approach to your communication as a healthcare manager means that you will consciously choose to see each communication encounter as a four-step process. Just as in any other strategic planning situation, there are clearly defined steps that you can use as a framework for thinking about the process, keeping in mind that the reality of individual situations can be considerably messier. This proactive approach, however, can reduce this sloppiness and unpredictability considerably.

The key questions delineated in our scenario offer a starting point for determining the four steps: research, plan, implement, and evaluate.

Research

The first step is, of course, research. Most strategic planners call the result of the research a situational analysis. But research is a broader term that encompasses the simplest to the most complex communication challenges. The amount of data gathering and analysis that you will need to do varies widely in communication situations.

For example, as a healthcare manager, you face every day what you might be tempted to refer to as routine correspondence, whether it comes via the postal service, your e-mail account, or even voice mail. Most managers have devised ways of dealing with such routine communication, and, luckily, these routine approaches often have good results. Sometimes, however, the results are less productive than they could be, or even cause further problems of which you may not be aware. I am not suggesting that you need to embark on a complicated research process for every piece of correspondence that you have to deal with, but what is required is an internalized process for quickly gathering and analysing the information you need. Here are the questions that should be in your mind as you deal with any communication situation:

- Who is this person or organization?
- What is their agenda?
- What is this person or organization's relationship to me and/or my organization?
- What other persons or organizations have relevant relationships?
- How important is the issue? How important could the issue become?
- Have we encountered this before, and what did we do about it?
- If it is a real issue that we/I have not faced before, are there others who have, and what can we/I learn from them?

The answers to these questions will provide a basis for dealing with everything from e-mail questions from potential clients/patients to a phone call from a reporter after allegations of staff misconduct. You should also be able to see where the issue of the so-called domino effect is beginning to emerge. You are not simply communicating with a particular individual or organization, but potentially with a whole host of others who might be affected by how you deal with the situation.

Plan

After you have established the basics, you need a plan of attack for dealing with the challenge, regardless of how simple or complex it might be. Whether you need a written plan or just the one in your head depends on a number of factors, including the complexity of the situation, the extent of its potential ramifications, and your own skills in using the particular communication mode.

Generally, the more complex the situation and the greater the significance of the outcomes, the greater the need for a written plan to which you can refer at a later date if necessary. Most important to consider, however, is the state of your own communication skills using different modalities (we'll examine those in detail in the next few chapters). For example, if you believe that your writing skills could use some work (or someone has pointed this out to you), then you probably need to begin to outline your work before you write even a simple e-mail. This outline is your plan. If your interpersonal skills are your weak link, you need a written plan prior to meetings. Everyone needs a written plan prior to making a public presentation whether at the chamber of commerce luncheon or at a press conference.

The plan, however, needn't be too complex: the simpler the better. All it really needs to include are the following:

- a few considerations about who this person or organization is,
- what you would like to accomplish,
- a clear statement of your message, and
- a few thoughts about the best medium to convey this message.

If we focus on the last point about medium, it may be worth considering a few issues. If the message came to you by mail, perhaps what you really need to do now is make a phone call or set up a meeting.

If you are having a meeting, you may also need to prepare a written document that will convey your message.

Implement

After you have considered your plan, the next step is to implement it. Implementing communication in health care involves your own personal set of skills in the areas of interpersonal communication, written communication, and public presentation. We will discuss these in some detail in the chapters to come.

Evaluate

Finally, you need to evaluate the outcomes of your communication. As you are sending that e-mail, forwarding dictation files to your assistant, or stepping down from the podium, you should think about how you will know if this has had the effect you intended. You need to consider both the extent to which you achieved your communication objectives and whether or not the effort contributes to on-going maintenance of the relationship with the audience. This smooths the way for future encounters. Communication doesn't end when the deliberate part of the process is over.

Communication and Your Mission Statement

Sometimes what you would *like* to say or write to someone is not really what is promoted in your organization's mission, philosophy, and values. Therefore, rather than thinking about how this hampers your ability to communicate in the way you see it, your organization's mission is better viewed as a kind of blueprint for the tone and direction of your communication processes.

Different kinds of health-related organizations have different kinds of missions. While issues of caring and curing may be part of many, this by no means represents the whole of what healthcare organizations do. Although this is not news to healthcare managers, the fact that these statements might have implications for strategic communication might be more novel. We will look at some examples of mission statements to see how these might help in the strategic approach to healthcare communication.

First, examine the following missions of several large, tertiary care institutions. Although there are similarities, as one would expect, they are not all exactly the same. Therefore, the relationships that they define vary slightly, setting different tones for their communication processes.

Mission Statement 1: Massachusetts General Hospital, Boston

> Guided by the needs of our patients and their families, we aim to deliver the very best health care in a safe, compassionate environment; to advance that care through innovative research and education; and to improve the health and well-being of the diverse communities we serve.[4]
>
> – Massachusetts General Hospital, Boston

Massachusetts General Hospital is clear about the importance not only of individual patients, but also about the patients' families and the position of the community. In addition, research and education, which are to be expected of tertiary care facilities, are also clearly stated in the mission. These are aspects of what they do that need to be front and centre in making decisions about how managers will communicate with both internal and external audiences.

Mission Statement 2: Hospital for Sick Children, Toronto

> As innovators in child health, we will lead and partner to improve the health of children through the integration of care, education and research: Providing the best in complex and specialized family-centred care; Creating groundbreaking scientific and clinical advancements; Engaging in knowledge translation and sharing our expertise globally; Enhancing an academic environment that nurtures experts in child health; and Championing an accessible, comprehensive and sustainable child health-care system.[5]
>
> – Hospital for Sick Children (Sick Kids), Toronto

The Hospital for Sick Children in Toronto, Canada, is also a tertiary care facility, but one with a narrower patient population. Their mission clearly focuses on that population as well as broader functions such as contributing to a sustainable child healthcare system. But, just as with the previous one, the elements of care, research, and education are a consistent part of the mission.

Mission Statement 3: St Jude Children's Research Hospital, Memphis

> The mission of St Jude Children's Research Hospital is to advance cures, and means of prevention, for pediatric catastrophic diseases through research and treatment. Consistent with the vision of our founder Danny Thomas, no child is denied treatment based on race, religion or a family's ability to pay.
>
> – St Jude Children's Research Hospital, Memphis

St Jude Children's Research Hospital,[6] in Tennessee, while providing care for a similar patient population as the Hospital for Sick Children in Toronto, has a slightly more focused mission that points directly to its role in finding cures for catastrophic childhood diseases. In addition, the hospital's founder and his personal story will have to influence both internal and external communication.

As we move from tertiary care facilities to examine the mission statements of smaller hospitals, Griffin Hospital in Connecticut (a 160-bed, acute-care community hospital) provides a good example of a communication approach that needs quite a different tone than the previous ones.

Mission Statement 4: Griffin Hospital, Connecticut

Griffin Hospital's mission is:

- to provide personalized, humanistic, consumer-driven health care in a healing environment
- to empower individuals to be actively involved in decisions affecting their care and well-being through access to information and education
- to provide leadership to improve the health of the community served.[7]

> – Griffin Hospital, Connecticut

The references to consumers and empowerment are clear in this sample, and will direct the nature of effective communication from a facility such as this one, and from its managers.

If we examine the missions of two different kinds of health-related organizations, it becomes even clearer how to use the organizational mission statement as a guide in the strategic process of healthcare communications.

Mission Statement 5: Shannex, Nova Scotia

We will lead the way to better living by: Providing the best care and service excellence to people as they age. We will achieve our Vision through our: Commitment to provide service excellence; Respect for clients' individuality and the choices they make; Pledge to protect their independence and dignity; and Promise that competent and caring employees continue to be the foundation of our organization.[8]

– Shannex

A group of long-term care facilities, Shannex, located on Canada's east coast, is not focused on research and cures, but clearly on nurturing. The messages regarding both the type of services provided and to whom the services are provided are apparent in all of the above mission statements—all clear bases for both personal and organizational communication efforts.

The next mission statement is representative of a different kind of health-related organization, and its message also provides tone and direction.

Mission Statement 6: American Nurses' Association

Nurses advancing our profession to improve health for all.[9]

– American Nurses' Association

A membership organization such as the American Nurses' Association (ANA) speaks to a different primary audience than do the mission statements of healthcare facilities. As a health-related organization that represents health professionals, their contract with society as documented in their mission statement describes a different kind of relationship, and therefore will require a different approach to communication. The ANA has embraced the tag line as mission statement approach and has distilled its mission into a statement that might be remembered by all who work for them.

Mission Statements as Communication Drivers

Most managers who have obtained masters-level education in business administration of healthcare management tend to see mission statements only in their most strategic function. They often fail to see the relationship between the statement and the tone, style, and content of the statement to both internal and external communication. That is not to say that communication is not strategic; rather it is to point out that there is a direct relationship as well as an indirect one.

The organizational mission statement assists us in the development of a strategic approach to communication in a number of ways.

First, when they are written well, mission statements provide a good understanding of the most important audiences with whom a manager will be required to communicate. Although they clearly don't provide an exhaustive list of constituencies, they do set the priority, provided the mission is a working document and not a pretty picture to hang on the lobby wall.

Second, mission statements set the priority for what an organization does. Often this can be useful when dealing with a communication issue that seeks to have the organization carry out a role for which it is not suited.

Finally, and most important from a communication perspective, the mission statement *sets the tone for communication* and even provides a certain level of vocabulary. If the tone set by the mission is not what the organization sees as appropriate, the mission statement needs revision.

If you examine your own organizational mission statement, what kinds of words do you see? If you have never looked at the mission from this perspective before, some of the words may lend themselves to your own communication efforts by setting the tone and providing some inspiration when you are searching for the right words:

quality	empowering
excellence	community
future	respect
compassionate	advance
leadership	enhance
personalized	image
humanistic	rights

Communication and Corporate Culture in Health Care

Although organizations have clearly had "personalities" since people began organizing, the term "corporate culture" has only actually been a part of our vocabularies since the early 1980s. Since that time, among both academics and managers, there has been increasing interest in attempting to understand the organizational behaviours that go beyond those that are most easily explained by either economics or logic. The study of corporate culture has been the result of this rumination, and organizational mission statements, with their tone and direction, lead to the question of how this cultural phenomenon might relate to managerial communication.

In large measure, the extent to which organizations, including both not-for-profit and for-profit, are able to achieve their missions, depends largely on how they are able to communicate this vision to their employees and eventually to their important external audiences. What is interesting here is that an organization's communication is both a product of the type of culture it exhibits as well as a creator of that culture. Thus, your own communication style as a manager is having a direct effect on the type of the communication climate in your department or institution, the culture that showcases that climate, and ultimately the extent to which you are able to assist your organization to achieve its objectives. This simple logic underlines the importance of one manager's communication skills and attitudes.

Obstacles to Communication

Despite planning, communication plans can go awry and fail to accomplish even the most modest objectives for the communication encounter. There can be any number of reasons for even the best-laid plans to falter. One of the most glaring is the failure to take into account the potential obstacles when planning what we intend to say and how we intend to say it.

One way to categorize these obstacles is to identify those that are related to the sender of the message, as well as those that are a function of the receiver. Perhaps a more useful way to think about these, however, is to make a checklist for examining a failed communication encounter. When you are examining the fallout from an unsuccessful communication effort—whether it is a meeting that didn't meet the mark, a presentation that seemed to not be well received, or a newspaper article that has misinterpreted your statements – the answers to the following questions may help you to pinpoint the obstacle that you failed to consider at the outset.

Communication Obstacle Checklist

✓ Do I respect both the audience and the medium?
✓ Was I anxious about any aspect of the encounter?
✓ Are my own skills in this kind of situation as sharp as they should be?
✓ Was I as prepared as I should have been for this communication encounter?
✓ Did I have enough information about my audience?
✓ Does this audience respect me and/or the organization I represent?
✓ Does this audience believe that I am credible?
✓ Does this audience have a sufficient level of interest in this subject?
✓ Does this audience possess the skills necessary to use the medium I selected?
✓ Does this audience have access to the medium I have chosen?

If you answered "no" to any of the questions on the checklist, you may want to explore that issue more. If you answer "no" to the same question in a number of unsuccessful communication situations, you have probably pinpointed one of your own personal issues with communication.

Carved in Stone?

A strategic plan for communication – whether for a large-scale organizational effort or a personal daily communication encounter – must be dynamic. A static plan, which looks good on paper but is not subject to change, fails to recognize that situations can and do change. As you gather more information, you may need to alter aspects of your approach for any of the following reasons:

• You may need to change your message if new information has altered the sense of what you are saying.
• You may need to change how the message is worded if new knowledge about your audience will affect your message.
• You may need to select another medium if the chosen one is inaccessible, too expensive (either for you or your audience), or of little interest to your audience.

These are some examples of modifications that may need to be made. As you consider changes to your plan of attack for a communication encounter, you create concrete data upon which to build the next approach.

Chapter 2 Key Points

1. Healthcare managers should realize that to be effective, communication at all levels needs to be the result of a strategic process.
2. Many organizations experiencing problems in their relationships with both internal and external groups may be using reactive rather than proactive communication strategies.
3. Each communication approach should be the result of having collected enough data from which the plan of attack was developed.
4. Each communication encounter requires an evaluation at some level.
5. Organizational mission statements provide clues to strategic communication by indicating both underlying message and tone.
6. Managerial communication in healthcare organizations contributes to the development of a culture that supports goal achievement or lack of achievement.
7. All strategic approaches to communication encounters need to be flexible and subject to change as a result of feedback.

For Your Bookshelf

Ferguson, Sherry Devereaux. *Communication Planning: An Integrated Approach.* Thousand Oaks, CA: Sage, 1999.

On the Web

The International Journal of Strategic Communication (an online journal). http://www.tandfonline.com/toc/hstc20/current?cookieSet=1.

3 Interpersonal Skills

We are what we repeatedly do; excellence, then, is no act, but a habit.

– Aristotle

What do your own personal habits say about you as a communicator? What do they say about you in your role as a representative of your organization or of your industry? How much do you rely on the communication skills of others without giving a lot of thought to your own skills? In short, how do you stack up?

In this chapter, we will begin our exploration of your communication skills by examining important aspects of interpersonal communication as well as some healthcare management situations where these person-to-person skills are key. According to executive coach Dr Patricia Wheeler, "Studies say 90% of executive failures are attributable to interpersonal competencies ..."[1] By the end of the chapter, you should have increased insight into your own level of skills in this area.

A Personal Thing

Defining interpersonal communication as a concept has become more difficult as communication technology has become more complex, yet, at the same time, more accessible. Many communication theorists believe that this dyadic form of communication isn't really all that different from other levels of communication (i.e., group, organizational, and mass communication). In fact, if you examine these levels closely, it seems clear that there are elements of the interpersonal in each of them. For example, whenever you attend or chair a group meeting, your one-on-one skills are very important. When you are being interviewed by a newspaper reporter, although your message will ultimately end up in the mass media, there is little doubt that your own interpersonal skills will be an important factor in your success at using the reporter as the conduit through which your message must initially pass.

So, although purists might consider interpersonal communication as an in-person, dyadic encounter, the skills you display in this kind of situation will clearly enhance or detract from your abilities in a much wider variety of communication situations.

Three important elements that affect any situation in which you must communicate with another person on an interpersonal level are as follows: your relationship with that other person, aspects of the two communicators (the receiver is also a communicator), and the dialogue itself. Let's begin by examining the relationship between you and your partner in communication.

Up, Down, and Across

It is very difficult for anyone in our society to spend much time without facing situations requiring interpersonal communication – and it is truly impossible for healthcare managers to do their jobs without it, regardless of their level in the hierarchy. Approaches to communicating in this one-on-one fashion, however, differ depending upon both the formal and informal relationship you have with the receiver of your messages.

One way to consider the formal relationships that provide a framework for your interpersonal encounters is to examine a formal reporting structure such as your organizational chart. Your interpersonal communication differs in a variety of ways depending upon your formal relationship with the other person.

Figure 3.1 is an example of a typical hierarchical organizational chart – the chart that is designed for public consumption. Although as a trained manager you might think that you already know all that you need to know about what an organizational chart can accomplish, it is likely that you have not given a lot of thought to the way it does or does not illustrate the reality of communication lines in your organization.

For example, if you are communicating with employees over whom you have authority, this will colour the encounter. How they perceive your management style will provide the backdrop against which

Figure 3.1 Typical Hierarchical Organizational Chart

```
                        ┌──────────┐
                        │   CEO    │
                        └──────────┘
                ┌──────────┐  ┌──────────┐
                │   PR     │  │  Legal   │
                │ Counsel  │  │ Counsel  │
                └──────────┘  └──────────┘
 ┌────────┐ ┌────────┐ ┌─────────┐ ┌───────────┐ ┌────────┐
 │   VP   │ │   VP   │ │ Chief of│ │    VP     │ │ VP HR  │
 │ Admin  │ │Clinical│ │  Staff  │ │ Financial │ │        │
 └────────┘ └────────┘ └─────────┘ └───────────┘ └────────┘
 ┌────────┐ ┌────────┐ ┌─────────┐ ┌───────────┐ ┌────────┐
 │Manager │ │Manager │ │ Manager │ │  Manager  │ │Manager │
 └────────┘ └────────┘ └─────────┘ └───────────┘ └────────┘
```

they will interpret your messages, for better or for worse. In the end, however, you will inevitably be interpreted in the context of your authority.

On the other hand, when you are communicating with those on your own level, even if they personally feel either above you or below you (in terms of expertise), they know that they are your peers. A formal lateral relationship is different than a vertical one and has an impact on the tone of interpersonal communication.

Then, of course, there is the informal relationship. These informal relationships can be a result of a variety of conditions, including:

- preexisting relationships (such as a family tie or a college roommate),
- current social interactions,
- your preconceived notions of someone else's relationships, or
- your preconceived opinions about someone's expertise.

Now compare the next organizational chart in Figure 3.2 to the previous one (Figure 3.1). This is how it might really work. You can see that the hidden parts of the chart can have considerable influence in the tone, style, content, and direction of communication.

Unfortunately, using an organizational chart is not useful at all when you consider your relationship with people outside your organization. They, however, will also judge your message based on where they

Figure 3.2 The Reality of Communication in an Organization

believe you sit: above them, below them, or on the same level. The criteria that individuals may use to determine your relative level include perceived expertise; perceived experience; age; gender; educational level; and sometimes even race, as much as we like to consider that we've evolved beyond this. On the other hand, these are the same criteria by which you subconsciously determine where others sit in relation to you as well. The bottom line is that the better you really know the person with whom you are interacting, and the more accurately they perceive you, the fewer obstacles you will encounter in the interpersonal exchange. The important lesson here is that even when you are communicating in a simple dyadic structure, you still need as much information about your audience as possible.

The Good, the Bad, and the Neutral

Not only do you have to consider horizontal and vertical relationships, you will also need to examine closely the quality of the relationship that you have with others.

If you have a long-standing, positive, productive relationship with someone – which is your goal – you will have little difficulty developing a rapport, even in situations where you might find yourself on opposite sides of an argument. This implies that every encounter you have with any individual will have potential consequences on the kind of communication that you can affect when the need arises. A person with whom you have a positive relationship will cut you a bit of slack when the going gets tough.

On the other hand, you may have cultivated negative relationships (or in fact failed to cultivate a relationship at all). A negative relationship is often characterized by an apparent lack of common ground. It can develop insidiously as you inadvertently deal with individuals without giving overt consideration to the long-term consequences of each encounter that you have. A negative relationship has a significant effect on the way each encounter is perceived. Often, the attitudes are unfavourable from the outset, regardless of the topic under discussion. This kind of interpersonal relationship can make achieving goals much more difficult and time consuming than necessary. If you take a few minutes to consider the individuals with whom you have personally negative relationships, you will recognize that if the relationship itself were improved, finding common ground and a positive starting point would be much easier.

Finally, you probably have a great number of encounters where you either have no relationship or a relationship that you can only classify as neutral. This is at least preferable to the negative relationship. Sometimes, it is to your advantage to maintain your neutral relationships, but you will encounter many individuals with whom it would be to your benefit to proactively cultivate a positive one.

Myths about Interpersonal Communication

Your beliefs about communication, in general, and your own skills, in particular, have an enormous effect on your success or failure as a communicator. Here are some commonly held beliefs that are, in fact, myths.[2]

1. *People pay attention when you speak to them.* Unless the other person is really interested in what you are saying (this means they have a personal stake in it), he or she is likely not really paying attention at all and certainly not to the extent that you may believe. One telling piece of trivia: a human being is said to absorb 600 to 1,200 words per minute when, on average, we speak at about 150 words per minute. If you do the math you realize that listeners have time to fill in the gaps with their own thoughts, rather than giving you their full attention. Do you always pay attention when someone else is talking to you? Or do you occasionally think about your next meeting, your grocery list, or your child's report card?

2. *If you think something is important, others will, too.* This could not be more untrue. You have to be able to express how the issue affects the other person and have that other person buy into it. This takes more than your enthusiasm (or anger, outrage, or intensity). It takes a good deal of researching in advance to determine how the other person might actually be interested in the issue, then creating your message to begin on common ground.

3. *When people nod their heads in agreement, they really have understood and agreed with you.* Wrong again. Nodding means nothing. A nod is no more or less than a gesture of acknowledgment that you are saying something – what that something is may or may not be understood. Further, the listener is showing neither agreement nor disagreement.

4. *When people say they understand what you have said, they do.* More frequently, that person will go away and begin to think about what you have said (if it is important enough to think about). Once away from you, the other person will find many other factors that will have an effect on what you have said, but you won't be there to address them.

5. *Repeating yourself is a good way to ensure that the listener understands.* Wrong. Saying something over and over, even using different words, is a very common and ineffective way to get your message across. Parents do it all the time, and so do bosses.

6. *Using emotional outbursts, including saying something more loudly, ensures that the listener receives your message.* If the listener did not understand what you were trying to say when you said it in a more modulated tone, speaking loudly or getting overly emotional will negatively affect your relationship and how the other person perceives your message.

7. *Using extreme gestures will get your point across better.* Pounding your fist on the table is a good example of this kind of gesture. It has the same effect as yelling (see item 6), which means that it can be perceived negatively and turn the listener against your message.

As you climb the ladder of managerial success, you might think that your position affords you some kind of special situation regarding these myths. Your subordinates may be forced into situations where you are attempting to communicate with them, but if you haven't taken the time to cultivate more positive relationships, they are no more likely to receive your messages than if you were on the same level as they are.

Cultivating Positive Relationships

How do you cultivate a positive relationship with another person with whom it is imperative that you communicate? Let's begin with a quick inventory of your own communication style. Look at the checklist in Table 3.1. Check off as many of these behaviours as you believe you have ever exhibited in the specified interpersonal encounters.

If you check off even one, think carefully about whether that exhibition was a one-time incident or a pattern of behaviour. If you find yourself checking off *any* of these behaviours, you probably realize that they are not conducive to successful interpersonal communication.

You may believe that yelling and pointing fingers (or pounding on the desk) are necessary in some situations, but they are not. This is an aggressive display that fails to lead to the kind of rapport that will allow you to meet your strategic goals. Whining and crying can be perceived as passive-aggressive behaviour, while condescension is not high on the list of ways to win support either. Refusing to respond makes you resemble a stone wall, while interrupting and over-talking can signal a number of underlying issues such as self-centredness, not listening, or simple rudeness.

If any of these are part of your interpersonal toolbox, you need to take a good, hard look at your relationships with other people. In addition, you may notice that you are more likely to exhibit a certain kind of negative behaviour in a specific kind of situation. This will need to be monitored so that you can replace the negative behaviours with more

Table 3.1 Behavioural Checklist

Behaviour	In Person	On the Phone	At a Meeting
Yelling			
Finger pointing			
Making digs or jokes			
Crying or whining			
Being condescending			
Refusing to respond			
Interrupting or over-talking			

positive ones. There is an old proverb that may help you to begin this process: "I not only speak so that I can be understood, but so that I cannot be misunderstood."[3]

Negative interpersonal behaviour contributes to unintended messages that may lead people to misunderstand your message and your motives.

Your Meeting Style

Do you have to go to a meeting today? Do you have to chair a meeting? Welcome to the wonderful world of management! Interpersonal communication skills are the key to your potential for attaining strategic goals through meetings. The question is this: what kind of interpersonal style comes through when you are participating in a meeting?

Generally, the positive interpersonal behaviour that we have been discussing is a good basis for achieving your objectives in the context of a meeting as well. Meetings, however, have their own set of rules, and what is acceptable in some interpersonal situations may not be acceptable at a meeting (or vice versa).

Acceptable behaviour at meetings varies considerably from one industry to another, but health care tends to be somewhat more conservative than, for example, the advertising business. In addition, meetings with various groups have their own dynamics and their own codes of conduct. For example, a meeting of the medical staff is likely to have different dynamics than a meeting of managers. Factors that can affect these meetings are such things as how well the participants know each other, the extent to which they share similar backgrounds and an understanding of the issues being discussed, and the history of how well this group may have worked together in the past.

If you are a manager attending a meeting of a group of health professionals whose backgrounds you don't share, the way you are viewed by that group will affect the dynamics. For example, if you are an administrator and are attending a meeting of the medical staff, your presence may change the usual group dynamics, perhaps injecting a degree of formality that may not normally be there. Indeed, your relationship with individual members of the group, the direct result of your interpersonal skills, will be a key factor.

Another key interpersonal communication skill that you'll need to be effective at meetings – either as a chair or a member – is your ability to listen. Business author Shri Henkel divides listening skills necessary for successful meetings into two types: verbal listening skills and nonverbal listening skills.[4] Verbal skills are those that require you to be able to summarize, clarify, and reflect back. Nonverbal listening skills involve such things as body position and eye contact. Different groups can also interpret nonverbal cues differently.

In general, meetings in which most of the participants know each other well tend to have a more personal style. However, this personal style may be disturbed by a guest. When this happens, all participants need to take a careful look at how their informal behaviour may be interpreted. Thus, in these situations, more formal acknowledgment of meeting manners may be appropriate.

Remembering that everyone is important and truly being present in a meeting situation can be the basis for effective interpersonal communication in these situations.

Chapter 3 Key Points

1. Effective interpersonal communication is fundamental to the strategic achievement of a variety of managerial goals and is necessary for successful group and mass media encounters.
2. The current and past relationship you have with another person will have a significant effect on your ability to get your message across in interpersonal situations.
3. Every encounter you have with any individual, no matter how seemingly insignificant, will have a potential effect on the type of communication you can achieve when the need arises.
4. There are many myths about interpersonal communication, and managers must rid themselves of such misconceptions.
5. Negative behaviours such as yelling, finger pointing, stone-walling, or whining are not conducive to goal achievement in strategic communication.
6. It is important to understand other's viewpoints so that you can introduce an issue in a way that is important to them, ensuring that they will listen to, and try to understand, your message.

For Your Bookshelf

Lencioni, Patrick. *Death by Meeting: A Leadership Fable*. San Francisco: Jossey-Bass, 2004.

Petersen, James. *Why Don't We Listen Better? Communicating and Connecting in Relationships*. Tigard, OR: Petersen Publications, 2007.

Stewart, John. *Bridges Not Walls: A Book About Interpersonal Communication*. 11th ed. Whitby, Ontario: McGraw-Hill Ryerson, 2011.

On the Web

Effective Meetings. http://www.omafra.gov.on.ca/english/rural/facts/96-039.htm

Four Principles of Interpersonal Communication. http://www.pstcc.edu/facstaff/dking/interpr.htm

How to Improve Your Interpersonal Skills. http://www.youtube.com/watch?v=w97dR3OJB1k

Six Steps for More Effective Meetings. http://www.effectivemeetings.com/meetingbasics/6tips.asp

4 Put It in Writing

The difference between the right word and the almost right word is the difference between lightning and the lightning bug.

— Mark Twain

Surely every person who makes his or her way into a managerial position in health care has adequate writing skills. Surely everyone who has graduated from college or university can write better than the average person. If you believe what William Zinsser says about writing (and you should), then you know that "Few people realize how badly they write."[1] And many healthcare managers are guilty of this.

But the fact remains: writing skills are critical to a manager's ability to communicate on a number of very important levels. In addition, how you write says more about you than you may have intended to say. In this case, with apologies to Marshall McLuhan, the writing in the medium is the message.

As you read this, take a mental journey through your own shelf of reference books. You should own (and use) the following:

- a good dictionary
- a medical dictionary
- a copy of *The Elements of Style* (by William Strunk and E.B. White)
- a copy of *The Elements of Grammar* (by Margaret Shertzer) or a reasonable facsimile
- a good book on business writing

If you lack even one of these books, you probably haven't given enough thought to the quality of your writing. And writing is something that a healthcare administrator does every day. What's more, evidence supports the notion that people who write well, think well. In other words, if you can organize your thoughts and select appropriate words to succeed in getting your message across to your audience accurately, you are probably a clear thinker. In fact, some managers even use this as a kind of litmus test when hiring new employees whose job responsibilities require them to be clear thinkers.

If we consider when and where a healthcare manager's writing skills are tested, we develop a kind of snapshot of the manager's job. Here are just a few of the situations where your own writing skills tell important tales about you as a communicator:

- e-mail
- memos
- letters
- reports and proposals
- minutes
- opinion pieces
- annual report letter
- editing employees' work
- clearing news releases
- articles for the employee or donor newsletter
- speeches and presentations

And the list goes on. Even if you have public relations personnel and administrative assistants to help you with these pieces, are you always so confident about the quality of *their* writing that you sign as if you had created it yourself? If you are at a lower level in the organizational hierarchy, you probably have to do your own writing, and the quality of your written communication will have a significant effect on your ability to climb to a higher level in that hierarchy.

Thus, it is clear that your own ability as a writer is a critical managerial skill. Let's examine how we determine what good writing is and then assess your own abilities in this area: how do you stack up?

What Is Style, Anyway?

The notion of considering your own writing style may bring back memories, good or bad, from high school and university English teachers. They always seemed to be talking about style, usually related to a particular writer: Ernest Hemingway, Mark Twain, Jane Austen, or William

Shakespeare. And although you may have even developed a sense of the differences in the individual writers' styles, that seems years ago and miles away from a healthcare setting and the kind of writing that you are required to do as a manager. But is it really? That depends upon how you define style.

A dictionary is always a good place to start (especially when you are writing). Webster's defines *style* as the "manner of expressing thought, in writing or speaking: distinctive or characteristic form of expression."[2] This sounds very much like what your high school teacher was trying to impart to you as you studied English literature. It also has some information for us as we develop our skills in writing on the job. Style certainly is your manner of expressing thought in writing, but we need to add to this the notion of expressing thought for a particular audience and purpose. Unlike Hemingway and Twain, or your current favourite author, written communication in health care is done not simply to express the author's thoughts or tell a story, rather to achieve a specific purpose for a specific audience. (We will discuss this further later in the chapter.)

Another way of defining style, however, is a bit more pragmatic, and perhaps for our current purposes, even more useful. In 1919, English professor William Strunk Jr wrote and self-published *The Elements of Style*,[3] a book that has become like a bible to many writers. Some years later one of his students, E.B. White, added his name to the author list, and we have what is now reverently referred to simply as "Strunk and White," and often cited as the final word on style. Most of Strunk and White is devoted to considering style as "what is correct, or acceptable, in the use of English."[4] In other words, the correct use of grammar, syntax (word order), word choice, and punctuation are an important part of style. And the reality of writing in business and the professions is that correct writing says much more about you than simply whether you can make your point.

Have you ever received a letter (perhaps a cover letter for a job application) that was riddled with spelling and/or typographical errors? What was your first impression of that person? Are you even confident enough of your own grasp of style to be able to determine all the errors?

Good Writing Is ...

If you listen to the sound of your words – yes, read them aloud – you begin to get a sense of the style of your writing. Your style is your own unique way of expressing your thoughts. But this is not enough in work situations. Keep in mind that your own personal style isn't necessarily good writing. You can write whatever you want in your personal journal that no one else reads (and I highly recommend doing so), but your writing on the job must meet a litmus test of a different set of criteria. Here are some of those criteria by which you may judge the quality of your writing.

1. *Good writing is accurate.* Nothing can harm your credibility more quickly than when a reader finds that you have not been accurate. This is even more important in health care, where inaccuracies can have deleterious effects on people's health.
2. *Good writing is truthful.* Just as in everything else that you do, integrity is paramount. Truthfulness does not, however, necessarily mean telling everything. You need to be able to exercise judgment when you are disclosing sensitive information, or when you are approving the disclosure by others in your work group.
3. *Good writing is utilitarian.* When you are writing in business situations, it is important that what you write has a purpose. Just as you are too busy to read material that has no purpose for you, consider others – good writing is useful for you, the communicator, and for your reader. It is your challenge to ensure that what is useful for you is perceived to be useful by the receiver.
4. *Good writing is clear.* Vague, murky writing, choking on too many words, fails to achieve its goals. If you like to use big words in places where smaller ones will do, get over it. Be clear and concise at all times.
5. *Good writing is well organized.* As we discussed earlier, well-organized writing often signifies a clear thinker. Looking at this another way, clear thinking must precede any writing, and a good outline helps to organize.
6. *Good writing is complete.* There is no point in writing something if you are not prepared to provide all the required details to ensure an appropriate response. Make sure the reader has all the necessary information to understand your message.
7. *Good writing is targeted.* Every piece of writing you do must consider its audience. Knowing who will read your message is just as important as the message itself, and should guide you as you write.

One final piece of advice on good writing has stuck with me since I read it somewhere many years ago. I believe that the most important rule of good writing is never to bore your reader. Although you might consider much of what you write to be mundane, day-to-day information exchange, you know that even an e-mail that fails to grab your attention in the first line or two gets only a skim from you, while an interestingly written one compels you to read it. Which scenario do you want played out on the receiving end of the e-mails that you take your own time to compose? As business writing coach Dr Wilma Davidson says, "Business writing at its best is a form of problem solving and calls for fresh thinking, imagination, and original, clear language."[5]

Different Styles, Different Purposes

What was the purpose of that memo you just wrote to your managers? Why did you e-mail a response to that family who was looking for information about their mother's hospitalization? Was there a reason for you to write that opinion piece in the local paper after their scathing series on local healthcare facilities?

There are many reasons for using written communication, and each instance has a unique purpose that you must consider before you write. The reason for the piece of writing has a huge effect on its style and on the outcome that you are likely to achieve. Both purpose and the resultant style, however, are also tied into the audience for the communication. We will discuss audience in detail shortly, but for now we will concentrate on answering the question "why" for each piece of writing.

Style

Three key components that differentiate one style from another are its pace, the tone that is taken, and sentence construction.[6]

Whereas each individual writer can develop his or her own style of writing, there are essentially four styles that we tend to use in healthcare situations.

1. *Business style.* This is probably the most commonly used style, and even it has variations. Business style is characterized by directness, relative impersonality, and speed of coming to the point. Effective business writing is fast paced, has a boardroom tone of voice, and uncomplicated sentence structure.
2. *Academic style.* You would have used academic style when you wrote research papers in college. In healthcare settings, you are more likely to read academic papers than to write them, but you need to be

aware of this style so that you don't mistake it for business or any other style of writing. (Indeed, if you are interested, you may find yourself collaborating on academic papers as well.) Academic writing is characterized by complete impersonality, remoteness, objectivity, detailed attribution, and a scholarly tone. Its pace is slower, and it tends to be more ponderous than business writing (although one might reasonably question why this has to be so – and the ubiquity of online academic journals does seem to be making a change in this), takes on a very impersonal, third-person style, and can contain more complicated sentence constructions. It presumes that the reader is highly educated and very interested in the subject area.

3. *Feature style.* Feature writing is the style that is characteristic of magazine writing (or, in the healthcare manager's case, the employee newsletter). In a modified form, it will also be useful for the fundamentals of a presentation, and sometimes in proposals or for opinion/editorial pieces. It is characterized by a relatively rapid pace, a familiar tone, and uncomplicated sentence structure.

4. *Personal style.* In healthcare situations, this kind of writing is usually appropriate only for written communication with individuals with whom you are well acquainted. It can vary in its pacing, has a first-person, personable tone, and relies on simple structures. In any business situation we need to be wary of too much familiarity and use this style judiciously. Extreme caution needs to be taken when creating e-mail correspondence in particular, where this style can easily creep in. Overfamiliarity has become the hallmark of social media communication among younger peer groups, and as they make their way into the work world including into healthcare management, they need to work hard at ensuring that this style does not creep into their written business communication.

It should be clear by now that each of these styles has a particular purpose and a specific target audience. You need to think very carefully about each piece you write before you write it – even when responding to what you consider to be routine correspondence.

Purpose

Written communication in the management of healthcare services and organizations has two main objectives. The first is a very simple, one-way approach: to provide information. The second is much more complicated than it appears on the surface: to induce someone to act.

1. *Providing information.* Arguably, providing information can be considered fundamental to any other objective one might have in communication. Indeed, it is difficult if not impossible to induce someone to take the action you desire if that person lacks clear, accurate, understandable information. This means that the better you are at providing information to a variety of different audiences, the better you will be at achieving your objectives.
2. *Inducing action.* The second objective for your written communication is to induce someone to take the action that you want or need that person to take. This involves perhaps even more planning and may require a number of steps.

Obviously, the first step is to provide the appropriate level of information, and at the same time to open a dialogue for two-way communication – feedback on the information received. This allows you to clarify and enhance. Then you move into finding the best way to get action.

Persuasion

It has often been said that there are essentially only four ways to get other people to do what we want them to do:

• payment
• patronage
• pressure
• persuasion

Your written argument could contain elements of any or all of these but essentially should be concerned with the last – persuasion – only.

First, you can, indeed, pay people to get them to do what you want them to do. In the case of management in health care, that approach usually means hiring. Enticing someone to do something by offering more money is a good approach under certain circumstances: if it is ethical, if you have no other option, and if you have the money. This is generally for only very specialized situations.

You could take the second approach and call in a favour. Patronage, in this sense, refers to convincing someone to do something for you because you have done something for them, or you might offer to do something in the future. This might work as the basis for your argument if you know your audience well and have a concrete, ethical foundation upon which to base this.

The third approach, pressure, could just as easily be termed coercion. It is highly ethically suspect as an approach because it has long-term, negative ramifications for your relationship with the person or organization on the receiving end. If your written communication seems to have an undertone of threat to the receiver, you are failing to consider the implications of your action, and you have not spent enough time considering how to develop the content of your written communication.

Although you may have been inclined to term each of the above persuasion techniques, in fact, from a communication perspective, they are not. You must consider changing how you think about persuasion. For our purposes, we can define persuasion as the use of communication strategies to change the way someone thinks about an issue – the pictures that person has in his or her head – so that he or she changes behaviour in the direction that the communicator wants. This requires you to consider the images that might be elucidated by the words that you select in your written communication.

Three ways of thinking about the persuasive words you select are using positive images, using negative images, or using logic.[7] If you paint a positive picture, you are inviting the receiver to move toward that image, to be a part of it. If you paint a negative image, then you are trying to make the receiver feel uncomfortable enough about it that he or she wishes to change behaviour away from that image. Finally, you may have an unemotional issue that does not lend itself to either a particularly positive or negative image. This is when you take Aristotle's approach and create a logical argument. It is often particularly useful to use this as a supplement to the more emotional approaches for long-term effect. Research on emotionally laden persuasion approaches has found that the results are fast, but short lived. Logic takes much longer to penetrate the mind of the receiver, but has more lasting effects.

The overriding objectives for all of your written communication should be to maintain and enhance a positive relationship with the receiver of the message.

Write for Your Reader

Throughout this discussion about what to write, when, and for what reason, we have continually hearkened back to the reader, the receiver of your written communication. The notion of knowing as much as possible about your receiver holds true for any kind of communication, but can be forgotten in the daily grind of completing our written communication requirements.

You have a number of audiences with whom you will need to communicate in writing, and each of them is different. They have different backgrounds, different levels of education, different types of relationships with you and your organization, and they have differing levels of interest in the topic about which you are writing. They also have different preferences for the medium used for receiving important information. Does your board request detailed reports? Do your colleagues favour letters? Do your employees prefer e-mails? Considering each of these factors is a key element in achieving your communication goals.

Myths about Written Communication

We all have certain beliefs about writing and how we write. Holding on to false beliefs can impede our success. Here are some commonly held myths about writing.

1. *Good managers are good writers.* Although this may, indeed, be true in some cases, one does not have any true relationship to the other. Many managers are particularly poor writers. In fact, there is no reason to believe that a manager will be any better at written communication than anyone at a lower level on the organizational hierarchy. Writing is a skill that must be consciously developed over time, and the only way to become a good writer is to write.
2. *If you can write for one type of audience, you can write for anyone.* Wrong. If you can write well for one audience (college professors, perhaps?), bravo. But suggesting that this can be extrapolated to other audiences has no foundation. Each audience has different needs (as we have already discussed), and you will likely find that writing for some audiences is easier and more satisfying than writing for others.
3. *Everyone who graduates from college or university has a good grasp of style* (grammar, syntax, punctuation, and word choice). When was the last time someone discussed placement of commas, semicolons, conjunctions, and the use of the subjunctive tense with you? For most college graduates, it has not been recently, unless you studied writing specifically. When was the last time you pulled out your style reference, or even your dictionary?
4. *Your reader is just as interested in your topic as you are.* This is almost never true, unless you are responding to something that originated with your reader, in which case it is more likely that you are less interested. Interest level is a very personal thing and something

about which you should gather information, especially when you are trying to persuade someone. For example, if you are trying to convince your board about an issue, you need to begin by determining how everyone feels about the issue before developing a persuasive approach.

Clutter

No discussion of effective written communication would be complete without reference to what William Zinsser calls the "disease of American writing."[8] That, of course, is clutter, and nowhere else – with the possible exception of government documents – is cluttered writing more sprinkled with jargon and unnecessary words than in healthcare communication.

Consider the following memo from the manager of an outpatient department to her booking clerks:

> In an effort to streamline the booking of appointments in the outpatient clinic, staff members are to be advised that the prioritization of patients will be completed prior to providing the patient with the appointment time. This will necessitate telephoning patients and advising them of their appointment times rather than being able to provide such appointment times during the initial telephone encounter.

What precisely does this mean? Look at all the unnecessary words. The truth is that the more unnecessary words there are, the greater the chance of misunderstanding. A less cluttered and clearer way to say this in a written memo or e-mail is the following:

> When patients call to make appointments, they are to be ranked in order of priority and telephoned later with their appointment times.

Different Formats, Different Rules

There was a time when the memorandum was the backbone of business communication. Everyone now accepts that electronic transmission of what used to go into memos has made a huge difference in how we use the written word to communicate. However, many people have altered their writing for electronic transmission with little thought about good writing for this specific medium. Clearly, different formats require different rules.

E-mail

Electronic mail has been a godsend to many busy executives. The quick turnaround that it requires is a huge advantage for efficiency (this in spite of the seemingly endless daily arrivals in the inbox). However, this rapidity has also caused some writing problems to sneak into such communication. Although e-mail is generally accepted to be less formal than other types of written communication, this can, and often is, taken too far. Here are some things to keep in mind.

- The subject line is extremely important. Ensure that it is clear, descriptive, and to the point.
- The body should have a salutation. Don't simply launch in. If you know the recipient well, you might begin with a simple "hello." Otherwise, "Dear ..." is suitable.
- Don't ramble on. Keep the message brief. Some people suggest keeping the length to the amount of text that can be read on the average screen without scrolling. Anything longer should be sent as an attachment.
- Use short paragraphs, and always proof the message before you send it! Typos are so common in e-mails, largely because many people who use e-mail are poor typists. Errors in e-mails provide the same subliminal messages as errors in other types of writing.[9]

News Releases

Although you may not be the one actually writing the news release, as a manager you need to be aware of the rules of this special format, because there is no doubt that you will have to approve them from time to time.

- News releases should contain news and not be sent on a regular basis. They should only be released when there is a specific, actual news item to relate.
- The audience for the news release may ultimately be the general public, but its first audience is an editor or journalist. Therefore, it should be written in newspaper style.
- News releases use the "inverted pyramid" structure. The most important who, what, when, where, and why should be in the first paragraph. The rest of the details can be filled in throughout the piece.

- News releases usually require a quote attributed to someone in the organization who is a credible source of information for the topic. It may be you.

Opinion Pieces/Editorials

As a healthcare manager it is very likely that you will be required to produce such a piece of writing at some point in your career. In fact, you should be looking for such opportunities. Here are some suggestions about this format.

- Select the media outlet for your opinion piece carefully. Ensure that the readership of the particular newspaper – whether printed or online – is a large part of your intended target audience.
- Write professionally, but personably. Keep your points clear and simple. Avoid jargon, but if you must use it, explain it.
- Keep the piece to between 600 and 800 words.

Newsletter Pieces

No matter what your level on the organizational hierarchy, you should consider the internal newsletter (print or electronic) to be an important venue through which employees can get to know you, and for which you can provide important information. You should seek out opportunities to use this medium. Here are some pointers for healthcare managers and their contributions to internal newsletters.

- Ensure absolute accuracy! This is a rule for all forms, but you cannot afford even one slip-up with your internal audience. Your credibility and future relationships depend on trust.
- Use a crisp, clear, uncluttered style. Avoid the use of adjectives and adverbs, and stick to the subject and its action. People do not spend a lot of time reading organizational newsletters, so get to the point whether printed or posted on the company intranet. Keep it short and simple.

Each of these kinds of writing (as well as any others you may have to do) has specific issues that govern their successful accomplishment. In the final analysis, however, the important thing is to ensure that your writing is readable.

Making Your Writing Readable

If no one reads what you write there is little point in writing it. As a manager you write to accomplish a variety of goals, not, like the creative writer, for the love of it. You may be able to bring a subtle artistic flair to what you write, but you must consider a number of concrete approaches that ensure your writing will be read.

The first rule of readable writing is to *simplify the complex*. Knowing your audience helps you to do this without insulting the intelligence of your readers. If you are trying to explain an upcoming merger to your employees, go one step at a time. Most healthcare workers will have had little business experience, and the process may seem complex and outside their realm.

Second, each individual element must be *coherent*. For example, as your teachers told you, the first (or topic) sentence of a paragraph indicates what that paragraph should be about. Writing that lacks this kind of coherence is difficult to follow and therefore not readable.

Third, select the *correct word*. Remember the Mark Twain quote at the beginning of this chapter? That says it all. C.S. Lewis added to this sentiment when he said, "Don't use words too big for the subject. Don't say 'infinitely' when you mean 'very,' otherwise you'll have no word left when you want to talk about something infinite." These days, there doesn't seem to be any word for what we used to call "awesome" since everything from your restaurant order to the Grand Canyon is awesome evidently.

Fourth, readable writing *uses as little jargon as possible*. Again, jargon use is related to the audience for your piece; however, you probably should consider your audience and then use even less.

Finally, readable writing *does not insult anyone*. Avoid sexism, stereotyping, ageism, and all other subtleties that may have a negative effect on anyone. Reread all your writing, and purge it of these negative habits.

When you have completed a writing piece, make a point of reading it out loud. You will begin to hear the sound of your words as mentioned earlier, and you will be able to pick up problems more quickly than if you simply read it silently.

Writing Resources

Because writing is so fundamental to communication, I want to make specific mention of writing resources. Countless books and Web sites are available to help you improve your writing. Listed at the end of the chapter are some of the more useful ones I have found, as well as several tests and crib sheets for your personal use.

Chapter 4 Key Points

1. Writing skills are critically important to a manager's ability to communicate.
2. How you write may say more about you than what you write.
3. In writing for healthcare management, style is your manner of expressing your thoughts to meet specific objectives for specific audiences.
4. The four styles of writing with which managers must be familiar are business, academic, feature, and personal.
5. One of the most important goals of managerial writing is persuasion, which can be defined as using communication strategies to change the way someone else thinks about a topic or issue.
6. The overriding objective for all your writing should be to maintain and enhance a positive relationship with the receiver of the message.

Writing Crib Sheet 1: Clutter

Don't use this ...	Use this ...
slowed down	slowed
in the near future	soon
at this point in time	now
at the present time	now
four o'clock in the afternoon	four p.m.
past history	history
very unique	unique
along the lines of	like
is in the process of planning	is planning
completely destroyed	destroyed
rose to the defence of	defended
be in need of	need
at all times	always
due to the fact that	because
give assistance to	help
in order to	to
make use of	use
make payment for	pay
on numerous occasions	often

Crib Sheet 2: Editing Problems

The following are some words that the not-so-trusty spellchecker on your computer won't pick up when used in error:

accept	except
adapt	adopt
affect	effect
appraise	apprise
canvas	canvass
complement	compliment
dual	duel
further	farther
grisly	grizzly
naval	navel
parameter	perimeter
pore	pour
reign	rein/rain
stationary	stationery
their	there
then	than

(If you don't know the proper usage of each of these words, now is the time to look them up!)

Test Yourself: How Does Your Writing Stack Up?

Section 1

Active voice is stronger and therefore almost always preferable to passive voice. Edit the following sentences to ensure that they're in active voice.

1. Control of the furnace is provided by the thermostat.
2. Fuel cost savings were realized through the installation of thermal insulation.
3. The policy manual is frequently updated by the supervisor's secretary.
4. Medical coverage in the emergency department will be provided by medical Emergency Specialists Inc.

Section 2

Purging clutter from your writing is essential to enhancing its readability. Rewrite the following sentences.

1. It is most useful to keep in mind that the term *Alzheimer's disease* refers to a whole spectrum of symptomatology.
2. It is unfortunate that I was unavailable to you when you visited our hospital facility on Monday.
3. It has come to the attention of management that there has been excessive smoking carried out by various employees close to the front doors, and thus we have come to the decision that there is to be a new policy that smoking within fifty feet of any doorway is to be stopped immediately and for the future.

For Your Bookshelf

Shertzer, Margaret. *The Elements of Grammar*. New York: Collier Books. (Any edition.)
Strunk, William, Jr, and E.B.White. *The Elements of Style*. (Any edition.)
Zinsser, William. *On Writing Well*. (Any edition.)

On The Web

The Basic Elements of English (U of Calgary). http://www.ucalgary.ca/UofC/ eduweb/grammar/
The Elements of Style (Strunk). http://www.bartleby.com/141/
Purdue University Online Writing Lab (OWL). http://owl.english.purdue.edu/
Theories about Persuasion. http://changingminds.org/explanations/theories/ a_persuading.htm
Twitter Tips: How to Write Better Tweet (Computerworld). http://www. computerworld.com/s/article/9132410/Twitter_Tips_How_to_Write_ Better_Tweets
Writing Effective E-mail. http://www.mindtools.com/CommSkll/ EmailCommunication.htm

Answers to the Writing Tests

Section 1: 1. The thermostat controls the furnace. 2. The installation of thermal insulation resulted in fuel cost savings. 3. The supervisor's secretary frequently updates the policy manual. 4. Medical Emergency Specialists Inc. will provide medical coverage in the emergency room.

Section 2: 1. Alzheimer's disease refers to a whole spectrum of symptomatology. 2. Unfortunately I was unavailable when you visited our hospital on Monday. 3. As a result of excessive employee smoking close to the front doors, smoking will no longer be permitted within fifty feet of any doorway. (Note that the use of the passive voice works here.)

5 Presentations That Deliver

The ability to speak is a short cut to distinction. It puts a man in the limelight, raises him head and shoulders above the crowd, and the man who can speak acceptably is usually given credit for an ability out of all proportion to what he really possesses.

– Lowell Thomas

It is often said that speaking in public is ranked as the number one fear of the average North American, outdistancing even the fear of spiders and snakes. Jerry Seinfeld probably put it best when he opined:

According to most studies, the number one fear is public speaking. Number two is death. Does that sound right? This means to the average person, if you go to a funeral, you're better off in the casket than doing the eulogy.[1]

If you are a healthcare executive, speaking in public is not an option – it is an absolute requirement to do your job well. Whether you are giving a presentation to an employee group, your board, a government agency, a community group, or your peers, speaking well can not only help you to achieve specific objectives for your organization, but it can also contribute to the development of your own career as a healthcare executive. Times have changed for speakers and audiences.

Some of the best books aimed at improving your public speaking are the old ones. Bert Decker, author of *You've Got to Be Believed to Be Heard*[2] suggests that the Winston Churchills of the world have given way to the Norman Schwarzkopfs – those who can command more than $60,000 for each speaking engagement because they are able to engage the audience's emotions.

Roger Ailes writes in his classic public speaking primer *You Are the Message* that one of the most common problems in communication is "presentation of material that is intellectually oriented, forgetting to involve the audience emotionally."[3] This means that the way you may have learned to deliver speeches may be outdated and ineffective with the audiences you will face today. (Making speeches and delivering presentations are two different things. Generally speaking, and with the exception of specific circumstances, stick to making presentations.) Today's audiences, whether employee groups or the chamber of commerce, are children of the television and Internet age, a fact that has changed the way they view entertainment, information, persuasion, and source credibility. And it is worth remembering that the granddaddy of all public speaking trainers, Dale Carnegie (who started teaching people how to overcome their fear of speaking in public in 1912) has this to say: "There is no such animal, in or out of captivity, as a born public speaker."[4] But even he could never have envisioned challenges that public speakers today face: audience members tapping away on tablets making notes, tweeting every nugget and texting others who aren't in the room.

We'll examine the why and how of making effective presentations that will enhance both your job and your career in health care today. Then we will examine how your personal skills stack up.

Making Your Presentations Strategic

Anyone working at any level of healthcare management must be able to make presentations. For some healthcare executives, making a presentation in public is as natural as brushing their teeth. For others, it is like a non-swimmer contemplating jumping off the back of a cruise ship – a terrifying experience that can and should be avoided. Between these two extremes is the majority that believes it is a necessary evil. But even mandatory presentations have a strategic component to them.

If we examine just the minimal qualifications necessary as a manager of any kind, it becomes clear that, even at this level, making presentations is a requirement. For example, it is now well established that front-line employees prefer receiving important information face to face (more about that in chapter 7) rather than in written memos, newsletters, intranets, or e-mails. This means that as a manager you are required to present informative and often persuasive messages to employee groups on a fairly regular basis even at very low managerial levels. Although these groups may be small for managers at lower levels on the hierarchy, as your career in health administration progresses, the size of these employee groups will grow as well.

Other areas within your role as a healthcare manager where presentation skills are increasingly important are in dealing with boards and government agencies. Often the healthcare manager is in the position of attempting to lobby or otherwise pitch something to these groups. Finely honed presentation skills are an important factor in the success of these efforts.

There may be some times when presentation skills may seem at first glance to be completely optional. However, for a career-minded professional, these seemingly voluntary situations are not. Whether you like it or not, as an administrator in health care, you are often viewed by the general public as a kind of expert in health care. While community groups may be inclined to see a doctor (or in some cases a nurse) as a health expert, you are a healthcare expert – and if your community doesn't see you that way yet, you need to take steps to place yourself in that position. This means that you may indeed have a responsibility to help others to understand the healthcare system, and as such will need to make yourself available to address interested community groups. This is increasingly crucial today as healthcare consumers are acutely concerned about the future of their healthcare delivery systems.

This has a two-fold result from your perspective. It not only provides much-needed accurate information for the general public, which can help your organization with its important messages, but it also serves to enhance your own profile in the community. This is beneficial both for the public image of your organization in meeting its community responsibilities as well as for your own image.

Other instances in which you may find yourself needing highly developed presentation skills include opportunities for you to bring your experience and expertise to your peers. Participating in workshops, seminars, and conferences for health professionals, trustees, and other healthcare managers provides you with an opportunity to give something to your profession, as well as to enhance your own professional profile in the healthcare community. Have you ever passed up these opportunities because you do not feel as comfortable as you would like to in making presentations? This is very common.

In this same vein, you may also have the opportunity to bring that experience and expertise to students in health care and healthcare management. Your skills as a presenter will allow you to respond positively the next time an instructor or professor calls seeking a guest lecturer.

Whether making presentations is required or optional, you still need to exercise some strategic thinking in selecting when and where to make those presentations. This decision derives directly from the objectives you have in making that presentation. For employee groups, you may be able to control not only the venue of the presentation but the size of the group as well. If you are bringing bad news, such as lay-off information, you may find it useful to make the groups small and the opportunities for immediate feedback greater. However, since the advent of social media, even if you provide opportunities for immediate, in-person feedback, many of the members of your audience will take to the Web to further provide reactions, and you need to be aware of this and follow up on it.

If you wish to make presentations to community groups, should you say yes to every request? Probably not. Should you seek out your own opportunities? Definitely, yes. In general, the presentations you make need to fit in with the overall objectives that your hospital or healthcare agency has for its relationship with the community (more about this in chapter 10).

In strategically selecting venues for public speaking, you should take a proactive approach. Don't always wait for situations in which you will be on the responding end. Consider the overall goals of your organization on an annual basis, and make plans to use your presentation skills to achieve specific objectives. Then, when you find yourself in a reactive situation, the audience that you face (the board or employees, perhaps), will already be familiar and positively disposed to your presentation style.

Preparation

The first rule of making presentations is to be fully prepared. This is one of the most effective ways to deal with stage fright. Even if you see yourself as a seasoned and comfortable speaker, never neglect this step. And while preparation involves more than making an outline of the topic to be covered, an outline is a good place to start.

Audience

As you sit down at your desk and consider what to say, begin by describing for yourself, in as detailed a fashion as possible, the audience you will face. The following questions may help you to tailor your presentation to this group.

- How does this group relate to you in terms of organizational hierarchy? This is always applicable when you are presenting to internal groups, and may be useful for some external groups.
- How familiar are they with this subject? The more familiar they are, the more appropriate it is for you to use related jargon; otherwise, avoid it entirely. You may also not need so much background if they already know it. Give your audience some credit.
- How interested are they in this subject? An audience that fails to share your enthusiasm for a topic area will especially need to be drawn into it emotionally, or they will tune out.
- How large is the group? The size of the group often dictates the degree of formality, the level of audience interaction you will be able to achieve, and the visuals you will need to prepare.

The answers to these questions will help you to determine a variety of factors including approach; language; tone; visuals; and, believe it or not, even what you should wear. But planning is key.

As Scott Berkun suggests in his funny public speaking manual, "The main advantage a speaker has over an audience is knowing what comes next. Comedians – the best public speakers – achieve what they do largely because you don't see the punch lines coming."[5] The only way that you can know what's coming before your audience does is if you plan it.

Openings

Once you are familiar with whom you will be presenting to and with your objectives for making the presentation, you are ready to begin preparing an outline. The place to begin is at the beginning. How will you start your presentation?

There are several approaches you can consider. Some people believe a joke is a terrific opener for a presentation. As a healthcare manager, however, exercise extreme caution in using this kind of an opening.

It might be a good way to start if (a) you know your audience well, such as your employee group; (b) the topic is a positive one (it may not be a good idea to begin with a joke just as you are about to inform them of layoffs); (c) the joke is carefully selected; and (d) you are capable of delivering a joke well (and this is not a universal skill). If all of these criteria are met, go ahead. Otherwise, you should select another way to break the ice.

Feature writers in magazines have a few ways that they usually start an article. These openings are just as useful in making presentations.

1. *Anecdote.* One of the most effective ways to begin to draw an audience emotionally into your presentation is to tell a story. The story should illustrate a human side of the topic and should be one with which this particular audience may be able to identify on some level. It can be a humorous story (which differs from a joke) if the topic is a light-hearted one. More often, when we are talking about healthcare issues, the anecdote is a more emotional one. It might even be a personal story, if it suits the topic, and can be a very good approach when speaking to your peers. The story itself should not be too long, but needs a beginning, middle, and an end. Occasionally, you might save the end of the story until the close of your presentation.

2. *Startling fact or provocative question.* This could be a statistic that is not likely to be known already by your audience; something that happened; a startling amount of money; something that is quick, to the point, and wakes up your audience. It can be very effective if selected well.

3. *Quotation.* Some speakers place the well-selected quote on a slide and let the audience read it while they are preparing to listen. This allows them a minute or two to absorb it before you begin talking about it. (This same approach can also be used when you use a question to begin your presentation.)

Whatever approach you choose to begin your presentation, you need to plan it in advance. Then provide the audience with a brief outline of what you intend to talk about on this occasion. Be specific about the purpose of the presentation and where you will end up at the end.

Occasionally it can be useful to tell the audience something more about yourself than may have been conveyed during your introduction (if you have been introduced). This is obviously unnecessary in internal presentations that are centred on day-to-day activities of your organization. If your audience is at all likely to ask the question "What the heck is this person doing here talking to us about this?" then you may need to present yourself and your credentials briefly. Ensure that this is not perceived as patting yourself on the back. It should not be self-congratulatory in any way, only informative, addressing any anticipated concerns of your audience.

Organization

The remainder of your outline should be the main points supported by the facts, information, and stories that augment each of them. There are various approaches to organizing material. The topic, objectives, and how you think about the subject will all play a role in which method you choose. Here are some of the methods:[6]

- *Topical.* Divide your subject into its component parts.
- *Chronological.* Topics that have a history or any kind of future timeline lend themselves to this approach.
- *Spatial.* You can map ideas using a visual aid.
- *Journalistic.* Organize the topic according to the who, what, when, where, why, and how.
- *Problem/Solution.* Select a problem for discussion and propose a solution.
- *Process of Elimination.* Eliminate alternatives and argue for the remaining option (especially effective when your presentation has a persuasive objective).
- *Motivational.* Use the psychological steps of gaining the audience's attention, establishing a need, satisfying the need, visualizing the results, and then providing some guidance for moving the audience to action.
- *Classical Judicial.* This is the provision of argument and counter argument, and again can be useful when persuasion is your goal.

Because a presentation needs a beginning, a middle, and an end, you need to outline your wrap up. Provide a brief summary, and then consider how you will actually end. If you haven't finished your beginning anecdote, then you have a ready-made ending. Otherwise, you may want to save a relevant quotation, a thought, or a call to action, if that is part of your objectives.

Appearance

Before we move on to considering your approach to the subject, it might be a good time to consider what *you* will look like. Although this may seem at first glance to be a frivolous matter for a serious healthcare manager, it is not. Today's audiences were brought up with a variety of broadcast and Web-based visuals, and are fairly sophisticated about drawing conclusions based on visual presentation. Most communications experts believe, and have evidence to support, the fact that most of us make up our minds about someone on first impression in about seven seconds. This means that how you look and the eye contact that you make will be either positive or negative input for the receiver of your message.

Deciding what to wear when making a presentation is actually just a marker for deciding how you will look to the audience in general, including the expression on your face and how much eye contact you make. Image consultant Catherine Graham Bell cites a great deal of research that concludes that, at least in job interview situations, personal presentation is the key factor in the decision about who will get the job and who will progress up the career ladder.[7] The same situation holds true when meeting people who are a part of your audience. They will make decisions about you before you even open your mouth. These first impressions can either help or hinder your ability to get your message across effectively. So, how will you present yourself?

As a healthcare manager, you represent a number of different constituencies besides yourself. Unlike the job interview where you represent only yourself, when making a public presentation you represent anything that the audience associates with you. This means that you are an ambassador for your healthcare organization, as well as the field of healthcare administration. Regardless of the venue or the audience you need to be perceived as a professional.

A good rule of thumb is to present yourself at one notch of formality up from that which you expect of your audience. If your audience will be wearing uniforms, you need to wear whatever you consider to be your best uniform. If you normally wear a uniform, too, this is what you should wear when making an in-house presentation at least (obviously a hospital-type uniform would be inappropriate at an outside conference). But your uniform should be impeccable, even if theirs are not.

If you are presenting to an external group or your board, you need to be just one notch up. If you know that the group is quite casual, you cannot be quite as casual as they are. Even if you choose to dress casually, you need to look well kept and professional. (By the way, if you are presenting at a conference where name tags are *de rigeur*, take it off before you take to the podium: presumably if you are up there, the audience knows who you are. And they are distracting.)

Your Approach

How will you approach your topic? What kind of a tone will you employ? Aristotle believed that there are three ways that we can persuade others to our point of view: ethos, logos, and pathos. These three approaches are useful in determining your tone and style even if your prime objective is to provide information rather than to persuade.

The first approach you might take is to simply rest on your laurels, but I do not recommend it. Aristotle called this *ethos* and indicated that the audience's acceptance of the speaker's message was dependent in this case on the believability of the speaker. Although this can't be the total basis of your approach, it may be a useful guideline in helping you to determine how much of your own personal experience can be used. If you are perceived by this group to be credible, you can capitalize upon this and use your own perspective as a basic approach. On the other hand, if you lack credibility in their eyes, you need to include something that will help to build that believability.

Aristotle's second approach, *logos*, rests on the strength of facts and statistics, all of which are used to put together a logical argument to make a point. Logic has a positive effect in the long term, but often fails to engage your listener in the short term. Thus, if a lot of facts and figures are needed to make your points, it might also be useful to consider a more emotional approach – what Aristotle called *pathos*.

Because communication technology is sophisticated and audiences are almost as sophisticated, the use of an emotional approach can be very effective. As we discussed at the beginning of this chapter, the reason Schwarzkopf was in demand as a speaker was not because of his ability to expound political rhetoric, or even to list facts and figures, but because he was always able to engage the emotions of his listeners. In the healthcare area, the potential for emotional connection is even greater than in many other areas. Indeed, health professionals need to guard against the very real possibility of exploiting this emotional hunger in audiences.

Each of these approaches on their own has limitations. Thus, in determining the approach you will take to a topic, you should consider including each of them in greater or lesser amounts. Your audience, objectives, and topic will dictate this.

Show and Tell

We take in messages through all of our five senses. In fact, some studies have shown that the relative effect of the five senses in the learning process is 11 per cent through hearing; 14 per cent through taste, touch, and smell; and a whopping 75 per cent through sight.[8] Australian speaking coach Doug Malouf says that a speaker is likely to achieve only 33 per cent of his or her goals without visuals, but 67 per cent with visuals[9] – a very compelling argument for always using visuals.

If we look at the history of humans making presentations, it's clear that visual aids have always been considered useful, whether that aid has been the Hebrew prophet Jeremiah using a ruined linen belt to make a point, or Cicero pointing out statues and landmarks to his audiences in Rome to illustrate his points.[10]

The reality is that you may not always be able to use visuals. It may be impossible or at least impractical to use visual aids when your presentation is very short, when you have been asked to speak in an impromptu situation (more about these situations later), or when the group is very small and intimate.

In general, your use of visual aids should increase proportionally with the size of the audience and the length of your presentation. A two-hour presentation to a conference of healthcare executives should make extensive use of visual aids, while a half-hour presentation to your board would include only a small number. Clearly, visuals are very important for your audience, but they are also important for you as the speaker. Well-designed slides not only reinforce what you are saying, but they provide you with a very clear outline for where to go next. Since you should never memorize a speech, they will guide you from point to point with very little shuffling of notes. There is nothing more impressive to an audience than a speaker who seems to need no notes—this goes a long way to enhance the speaker's credibility. In addition, shuffling through notes is often distracting for the audience. Use your visuals well and remember this caution from public speaking coach Richard Zeoli: "Do not make the mistake of relying on PowerPoint® or visuals to tell a story."[11]

It is time to turn our attention to the practicalities of visuals – how to select them, prepare them, and use them.

Selection

In selecting the format and tone of the visuals, you need to think about the same audience considerations that you used in the preparation of your outline: size, type, interest, and knowledge levels. While you might use light-hearted visuals for a casual topic with a peer group, a serious topic may require a more polished look. The format you choose will depend on functional considerations such as the room size, availability, and portability. There is no point in selecting a slide presentation in a room so small that the slides will look like your vacation pictures hung on the wall. If you are going far afield, you must be able to transport your visuals, so a flip chart might not be a good idea. If you are speaking to a community group, check to make sure they have access to an LED projector before you begin to prepare a computer-based presentation, and if you need a connection to the Internet, you need to be very clear about whether or not it will be available to you.

Presentation

How many times have you gone to a conference and been faced with a presenter whose visuals were impossible to see from the back, or so full of text that you couldn't even begin to read them? I have even passed classrooms where professors are using photocopied pages from books as transparencies – in the twenty-first century! Unfortunately, these situations happen more often than they should.

There is nothing more effective than a well-thought-out, well-designed visual. Here are my very basic design considerations when preparing visuals to accompany a presentation:

- select a format and colour scheme and keep it consistent (Your organization should have a branded template for slide presentations.)
- keep them simple and uncluttered
- keep the background clear
- ensure that the type is a significant contrast to the background
- avoid large text blocks at all costs
- use large enough type
- avoid overly ornate type faces

- use lines and clip art sparingly
- use graphs, flow charts, and photos when appropriate

An abundance of software is available today for developing visuals for presentation.[12] It is, however, only as useful as the user's grasp of basic design. Although many programs provide templates,[13] not all are effective in all situations. I don't know about you, but I am sick of poorly developed computer presentations. If you do not know how to develop and use visuals well, these computer-enhanced slides are not going to save you. If you are going to use this method or one similar to it, consider the following:

1. The less contrast there is between the type and the background, the darker the room has to be (and darkened rooms are more conducive to sleeping than to taking notes).
2. Too many swirl-ins and rotate-outs can leave the audience feeling dizzy.
3. The darkness allows much less eye contact with your audience.
4. Incorporate videos and other online material as appropriate. However, it's important that you know exactly how to access these the exact moment when you need them, and remember that using too many can detract from your own personal message. (And note the comment above regarding availability of Internet connections in the planning process.)

One final note about using visuals such as these: always manipulate your own slides. This avoids the need for continually interrupting your remarks with "Next slide, please!"

Never Make a Speech! (Well, at Least Almost Never)

Whenever I hear that someone is going to "make a speech" I immediately start to yawn. While a well-delivered presentation can be life changing, unless you are a Martin Luther King Jr, you should avoid making speeches except in the most specific of circumstances when the message delivered from a prepared statement may be crucial to ensuring accuracy of the message.

This may be a simple matter of semantics, but here is what I mean by a speech. Webster's defines a *speech* as "a public address; a discourse,"[14] and gives "a sermon"[15] as one of the definitions of a *discourse*. Need we say more?

One of the problems with speech making is that there is the tendency to read from a prepared text at times when such a delivery is inappropriate to say the least. When you are making a presentation, you should (a) never write out your entire presentation word for word, or (b) read from the prepared text. In fact, writing out a "speech" word for word increases the likelihood that you will, in fact, read it. This also means that you should never get your public relations staff to write a speech for you. You might, however, ask them to provide "speaking notes" that will provide you with a well-organized approach to the points you want to make.

Impromptu Speaking

For every professional there comes a time when someone unexpectedly says, "Could you just say a few words?" Then it is up to you to think on your feet and say something coherent and useful. The key to these unexpected situations is to never let them be truly unexpected.

It is usually possible to anticipate situations where it is likely that someone might make such a request: at a board meeting, at the annual dinner honouring your long-time staff, or at a public meeting considering your hospital's application for expansion. Consider those Hollywood stars who aren't sure they will win the Oscar, but they always prepare their acceptance speech. Don't ever let yourself be completely unprepared.

The best motto you could adopt for these and most other communication situations is to think before you speak. As you rise to move toward the microphone, do so slowly and deliberately, thinking all the time. If you follow the second rule – keep it short – this brief moment of preparation will be enough to carry you through. As some people begin to talk, however, they start to prattle. Listen to yourself and try to connect with your audience to avoid this.

Finally, one of the best ways to ensure that your remarks are coherent and have a beginning, middle, and end is to tell a story if you can think of one quickly. It will always be better organized than a series of disconnected remarks.

Collaboration: The Team Approach

Often, a team approach to a presentation can be a most effective tool for meeting your objectives. If a variety of expertise is required, you might consider a group of specialists. For example, if you are making a pitch for money to enlarge your emergency department you might consider asking both a physician and a nurse to present with you. If you are lobbying to change admission policies to your long-term care facility, you, your director of admissions, and even a family member might be a dynamic team. There are, however, some issues to consider when working as a team.

First, although each of you has a particular area of expertise, you need to organize the presentation as a whole. This means getting together to plan the objectives, approach, and tone. You also need to take an inventory of what each participant knows about the issue and the individual relationships with the proposed audience. This overall organization also extends to your visuals – they must be consistent. Once the planning is out of the way, the group should rehearse together and determine how you will handle the actual presentation and any question that will naturally follow.

One of the best tools you can use for developing a group presentation is a wiki. A *wiki*[16] is a collaborative Web site that a number of people can contribute to and that no one individual in the group owns. Each member can develop content, and each member can edit any content. The wiki also provides a history of the content edits and a discussion. If you do not have access to a wiki on your in-house intranet, you can sign up for a free one on a Web site such as Wikispaces (www.wikispaces. com). For a quick primer on how to use a wiki, see the Web resources at the end of this chapter.

There are two problematic aspects of actually speaking as a group. The first is the way transitions are handled. There should be a smooth lead-in to the next speaker by the previous one, and you need to consider carefully how the audience is likely to react to bouncing back and forth from speaker to speaker. It can be very distracting. In general, you should avoid organizing the material so that it is necessary for any one person to speak more than once, with the exception of the person who might open and close the presentation.

The second concern is figuring out what everyone else should be doing while one member of the group is speaking. The audience will see all of you, and if one of you looks bored or uninterested in what the others are saying, the audience will pick this up. When you are not speaking, you should pretend you are on camera at all times, because anything you do can and will be picked up by at least some of your audience members (who may find it necessary to tweet about it as you sit there!). Maintain your interest by unobtrusively nodding and making the occasional note. And never interrupt or correct the speaker!

Finally, you need to decide early on how you will handle questions. It is most appropriate for each speaker to handle questions, rather than having one do all the talking.

How Do You Stack Up?

Here are some questions that you might ask yourself to determine just how well prepared you are for making presentations.

✓ When asked to speak, do you always ask the following questions:

  ◦ How many people will be attending?
  ◦ Who will the audience consist of?
  ◦ What do they know about this issue?
  ◦ Whose idea was it to present about this topic?
  ◦ How large is the room?
  ◦ How is the room laid out?
  ◦ What kind of audio-visual equipment is available?
  ◦ Is there an Internet connection?
  ◦ How long will I be speaking?
  ◦ Will others be speaking?
  ◦ If yes, what will they be speaking about, and when will my presentation be in relationship to the others?

✓ Do you always spend some time thinking about how you will begin?
✓ Do you always prepare an outline?
✓ Do you always figure out what your objectives will be for the presentation (both for you and for your organization)?
✓ Do you always do more research than you think you will need?
✓ Do you always consider carefully the kind of visual impression that you will make on this particular audience?
✓ Do you prepare eye-catching, uncluttered visuals to support your presentation?
✓ Do you feel comfortable in the use of a variety of audio-visual approaches (PowerPoint, videos, audio)?

✓ Do you practice before the presentation – especially with the technology?
✓ Do you always speak approximately within the time that was allotted to you?
✓ Do you always avoid prattling on?
✓ Do you feel comfortable fielding questions?
✓ Do you ask to see any written evaluation that may be done by participants (e.g., at a conference)?

If you can honestly answer "yes" to all of the above questions, then you stack up well against your peers. If, however, there are areas that you have failed to consider or where you feel uncomfortable, you may need to think about your presentations a bit more or even ask for outside coaching.

You cannot avoid making presentations in your career as a healthcare manager. Indeed, it is to both your advantage and that of your organization for you to seek out opportunities to put yourself in front of an audience to meet strategic organizational objectives.

Leaving Your Presentation Legacy

Often it seems like after your presentation the work simply goes to waste. In the digital age, there is no need for this to happen. You can give your presentation a longer life and let those who were unable to attend the presentation an opportunity to learn from you by posting them on a slide-sharing site or narrating your PowerPoint™ presentation and creating a video.

The following online services support this kind of approach by permitting you to create a free account and uploading your slides and information about them:

- SlideShare (www.slideshare.net)
- AuthorSTREAM (www.authorstream.com)
- Slideboom (www.slideboom.com)
- myBrainshark (http://mybrainshark.com)

In addition, you can add narration to your presentations and create videos that can be shared via video-sharing sites such as YouTube and Vimeo.

However you choose to do it, you may find that having your presentations online may be advantageous to both you and your organization.

Chapter 5 Key Points

1. Anyone in healthcare management must be able to make presentations to meet strategic objectives.
2. Today's most successful speakers are those who can engage their audiences rather than simply produce a list of facts and figures.
3. The first rule of making presentations that deliver is to be fully prepared in advance for both your topic and the specific audience.
4. Always prepare an outline. Never write out the full text (you might be inclined to read it).
5. Visual aids greatly enhance the potential that you will meet your goals for any presentation.
6. Good visuals are consistent, appropriate for both the topic and the audience, and are used knowledgeably during a presentation.
7. Even when asked to speak extemporaneously, think before you speak, outlining in your head what you will say, and then keep it short.
8. To meet certain strategic objectives, it is sometimes most effective to use a team approach to presentation.
9. Keep the title slide simple and clear. This format could be in colour for slides or computer display, or overhead display. This landscape layout can be changed to portrait layout for overhead projection.
10. Provide a presentation outline in bullet format as part of your introduction.
11. The use charts can enhance the visual impact of presenting statistical information.
12. It should be clear by now that you don't want to place your entire presentation on your visuals.

For Your Bookshelf

Jaffe, C. *Public Speaking: Concepts and Skills for a Diverse Society*. 6th ed. Boston: Wadsworth, 2010.

Zeoli, R. *The 7 Principles of Public Speaking: Proven Methods from a PR Professional*. New York: Skyhorse Publishing, 2008.

On the Web

Allyn & Bacon's Public Speaking Web site. http://wps.ablongman.com/
ab_public_speaking_2/

An Unconventional Guide to Public Speaking. http://www.entrepreneur.com/
video/223160

Common Craft. "Wikis in Plain English." http://www.youtube.com/watch?
v=dnL00TdmLY

Graphics & PowerPoint with a Leadership Edge. http://www.homework
market.com/sites/default/files/barrett_chapter_6.pdfToastmasters
International. "10 Tips for Public Speaking." http://www.toastmasters.
org/tips.asp

6 Fundamentals of Social Media

We lived on farms, then we lived in cities and now we're going to live on the Internet!

— Sean Parker in *The Social Network*

Social media have changed forever the way that organizations communicate with their important publics, but it is much more than simply a new way of communicating. Its participatory nature and its ubiquity have resulted in nothing less than a transformation of not only how organizations of every stripe communicate, but also how they develop *relationships* with publics. There is little doubt that the notion of "controlling the message" is fast becoming an anachronism.

User-generated content has had enormous implications for communication outcomes to be sure; however, it has also had an impact on cultural considerations – everything from simply how we have become a culture seemingly void of privacy filters to the notion that we have, as Andrew Keen would say, seen the rise of the "cult of the amateur."[1] These are transforming the way we relate to one another. Healthcare managers require a substantial understanding of how social media are evolving, how people are using these tools, and what impacts these have on both cultural and communication outcomes

The Tools of the Trade

Facebook, YouTube, LinkedIn, Second Life, Digg, Pinterest, Twitter, wikis, blogs – the list goes on. These are just some of the tools that are currently available and widely used in the world of social media. It seems clear at this stage that the world of social media is here to stay, and it has become a very high-profile part of how organizations communicate and engage with their publics. However, questions abound.

- What tools are available, what is on the horizon, who is using these tools, and what are they using them to accomplish?
- How important are these tools to organizations today in general and healthcare organizations in particular, and what will be the importance in the future?
- Are you personally adept at using social media to enhance relationship building on an organizational level? On a personal career level?
- How are social media tools being creatively applied to healthcare situations?
- What would improve the use of these tools and tactics?

There are so many questions, and the fact is that their answers are a moving target. It is possible, however, to acquire the basic social media knowledge that healthcare managers need to move through its ever-changing landscape without making too many mistakes.

What Exactly Constitutes Social Media?

In some sense, the term *social media* encompasses everything that the term *traditional media* does not – but that does not quite tell the story. Social media truly is a bit like letting the inmates run the asylum to reiterate an oft-used simile. The audience takes charge of the content so that the content creator becomes the content consumer who then becomes the creator and so on.

Characteristics of Social Media

For our purposes, we'll define social media as

> online technologies and applications that are used to share information, opinions, expertise, insights and interests using text images, audio and video in a participatory environment.[2]

Figure 6.1 The Social Media Cycle

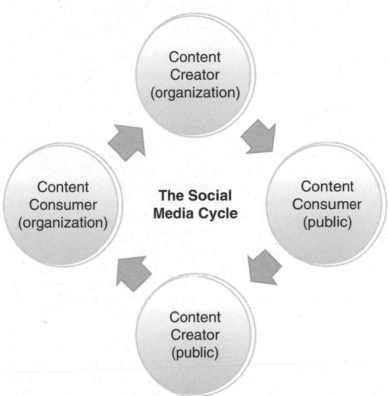

Social media tools all share several important characteristics. They are as follows:

- *A participatory environment.* True social media does encourage that participation piece. If you have a blog for example, and yet you choose to turn off the comments function thereby disallowing anyone to provide immediate feedback, your social media platform is not truly social. That being said, those readers who wish to comment will do so in other venues to which you might not have immediate access and which you might not even know about until it's too late. Once they take to Twitter, comments can and do go everywhere.

- *An accessible nature.* Accessibility to the tools available is controlled only by an individual's or organization's access to the Internet. Access to the Internet is increasingly considered to be a right rather than a privilege in our society.
- *Community generation.* As a consequence of the "social" nature of social media, the opportunity for community building has never been greater. Individuals collect around topics of interest to them, and a community is created – for better or worse from an organization's perspective.
- *An enhanced connectedness.* Never before have people, regardless of geography, in particular, been as connected to one another. This is both a boon and a burden. From an organization's perspective, being able to connect with important stakeholders can be a great advantage; conversely, as individuals, all of this connectedness can be overwhelming and invasive if not controlled.
- *Opportunity for dialogue.* Never before have healthcare organizations had such an opportunity to seek feedback and engage their various stakeholders in conversation. The extent to which this becomes true dialogue where active listening is a part of the equation is dependent upon the strategy within which the social media tool is used.

How people find information has changed dramatically. So too have the sources of information and influence changed. The old term "word-of-mouth" that has always held sway has a whole new meaning. In addition, social media use has drastically changed the role that individuals play in disseminating and influencing others. Healthcare organization can capitalize on this if they understand both the tactics involved and available, and the broader managerial perspective that is necessary for strategic deployment of social media tools.

Social Media in the Healthcare Community

It has been widely reported that online searches for health-related information are the most frequent query. It would be difficult to provide reliable data on the use of social media by healthcare consumers and healthcare providers since it changes daily; however, a quick view of some of the available information at this writing will put the importance of these tools and tactics into perspective.

Here are some interesting research findings:

- A pharmaceutical and healthcare research company reported in May 2011 that 75 per cent of American physicians own some sort of Apple device.[3]
- The same research company also reported in October 2012 that 73 per cent of American adults use online health information to assist with decision making.[4]
- Fifty-five million American adults (55 per cent of those with Internet access) have searched for health or medical information on the Web.[5] (Note: Some sources suggest that the number is closer to sixty-five million at this point; however, the number is a moving target.)
- In spite of the multiple millions of Americans who seek healthcare information on the Web, these searches are not covered by HIPPA (Health Insurance Portability and Accountability Act) regulations.[6]

These statistics provide for us a picture of the vast influence of social media in the healthcare environment, yet they do not yet provide definitive answers on how we might best leverage social media for improving health care. We are in the beginning stages of truly understanding how to use social media to actually improve health outcomes. In fact, "... compared to other sectors, healthcare organizations have been relatively slow to be comfortable with social media as a way to connect with patients" largely because there is a "lack of a set of accepted best practices that would enable organizations to become less risk-averse."[7] Only now are we beginning to see the beginnings of literature on best practices.[8]

A shared understanding of the best ways to use social media in the strategic management of healthcare organizations will no doubt have a direct impact on health outcomes in the future, but first you need to be fluent in the social media tools available.

The Tactical View

There are countless tools currently available in the world of social media. Just when you think you've mastered using LinkedIn, a new business-networking site comes online, and people begin flocking to it. And so it goes with all types of online social media tools. Developing a comfortable facility with these tools and tactics assists healthcare managers to conceptualize the bigger picture when faced with the managerial issues that we'll discuss later.

The "Big Eight" Social Media Tools

In spite of the plethora of social media tools in cyberspace and the fact that they are a moving target as we discussed earlier in this chapter, for discussion purposes it is possible to categorize these tools into eight groups as illustrated in Figure 6.2.

These are the eight general categories into which most tools and tactics can be grouped. Keep in mind, however, that the categories are not mutually exclusive, and some are hybrids of one another and when used together create a kind of mash-up.[9]

Figure 6.2 The Big Eight Social Media Tool Types

Blogs	• The ubiquitous online journals that are used by everyone from aspiring authors to CEOs
Microblogging	• Online updates typically in 140 characters or fewer (Twitter is the foremost example)
Social networks	• Web sites that encourage connection andcontent sharing
Content communities	• Collections of users who come together to share particular content (e.g., photos, slides, information on an issue)
Wikis	• Collaborative sites that allow users to add or edit content
Podcasts	• Audio or video files that are available for download (sometimes by subscription)
Forums	• Online discussion groups
Virtual worlds	• Web-based simulated environments where users interact as avatars

Here are some applications for these categories in the healthcare setting:

- *Blogs*

  - Establish the organization's expertise
  - Provide patient information and ask for feedback
  - Enhance participatory internal communication

- *Microblogs*

  - Provide brief updates, especially during a crisis
  - Quick information, especially on items that change

- *Social networks*

  - Connect with specific communities such as immigrant groups
  - Evaluate potential employees (controversial but an application nonetheless)

- *Content communities*

  - Patient education on specific health issues
  - Organizational reputation enhancement

- *Wikis*

  - Patient education materials that can be developed collaboratively and made available online
  - Project and group management

- *Podcasts*

  - Patient education
  - Internal communication

- *Forums*

  - Creating dialogue with community/patient groups
  - Enhancing employee participation in managerial decision making

- *Virtual worlds*

  ◦ A virtual world based on the exact specifications of your health-care institution can be effectively used for pre-hospital orientation for patients

These are ideas that can help to start those new to using social media for professional communication thinking about creative ways that the tools can be applied. It is important to understand, though, that none of these can be useful in isolation. Their use has to be carefully *integrated into both the overall business plan for the healthcare organization and the communication strategy*. This can only be done by taking a broader view as a manager must.

The Managerial View

Social media are neither simply the tools and tactics that represent them, nor are they simply reflected in the impacts that this new approach to communication and relationship building has on culture and outcomes. From our perspective in healthcare management, especially for those who will take on leadership roles, social media are also a managerial consideration. In the future, social media, and whatever it evolves into over time, will become increasingly important in how organizations relate to their internal and external publics. Using or not using these tools has impacts on the overall place of the organization in society, and has implications for managerial planning. Within this planning context, issues like ethics and legal implications are important considerations.

The key concepts that you need to understand before plunging into the use of social media in your organization are shown in Figure 6.3.

Once you have assimilated these key concepts, you need to remember that everything in cyberspace is forever. All organizations today also need to be aware that they ignore social media at their peril.

Social Media Policy

Every organization today needs to have a well-thought-out policy governing social media use by the organization and its employees. There are no exceptions. In addition, any social media tool you develop needs to have its own policies.

Figure 6.3 Key Concepts for Understanding the Organizational Use of Social Media

Social media tools and tactics have specific characteristics that make them different - not always better - than more traditional approaches to communication.

Just as in any other decision-making situation, youo need to be clear about what you want to accomplish before selecting the tools to use.

Not all social media tools and tactics work in every situation nor with every stakeholder group.

Social media tools do allow for a considerable degree of creativity in their strategic applications.

Before integrating social media tools and tactics into your communication strategy, your organization needs a social media policy in place.

Overall policy should include the following considerations:

1. The policy must be tailor made for your own organization, taking into consideration your individual mission in health care.
2. The policy needs to address aspects of confidentiality and privacy for all stakeholders. This is particularly important in health care when dealing with confidential health issues.
3. Employees need to be held to a policy that governs their behaviour when online. This means that they need to be aware that their behaviour might breach confidentiality or be embarrassing to their employer; therefore, your policy needs to include guidelines for online behaviour. This policy needs to govern their behaviour both at work and when off duty whenever they can be associated with you as their employer.
4. The policy needs to consider how the organization will handle on-site use of social media. Will you permit employees to use social media when at work? Will they be allowed to update their Facebook accounts, tweet, view videos? Likely not. Thus, the policy

needs to be clear about what is and is not acceptable during work hours.

Once you have this kind of policy in place, you need to consider policies for your specific social media tools. For example, the Children's Hospital of Los Angeles invites former patients to share their stories on a special part of their Web site. Their policy is clear about what is to be shared, what the hospital will do with the information, and how some of the uses may not be able to be controlled by the hospital once the material is posted.[10] For other examples of social media policies in a wide variety of organizations, visit the Social Media Governance Web site.[11]

This discussion has been but the tip of the proverbial iceberg when it comes to social media applications. Familiarity with these tools will allow healthcare mangers to consider a deeper reflection on how they will be best integrated into existing strategies to accomplish ongoing goals in the organization.

Chapter 6 Key Points

1. The participatory nature of social media and its ubiquity have changed forever the way that organizations communicate with both their internal and their external stakeholders.
2. Health and medicine are two of the most frequently used search topics on the World Wide Web.
3. It is important that every healthcare manager develop more than a passing knowledge of the social media tools and tactics available today and to keep up with what is developing.
4. In spite of what seems to be an overwhelming number of different social media tools, most can be categorized into one of eight groups: blogs, microblogs, social networks, content communities, wikis, podcasts, forums, and virtual worlds.
5. Many new social media tools are combinations of the above eight.
6. Social media tools cannot be developed and implemented in isolation from other aspects of the organization's strategic and communication planning.
7. Every organization needs a social media policy whether or not they are planning to implement the use of the tools.

For Your Bookshelf

Murero, M., and R. Rice, eds. *The Internet and Health Care*. Mahwah, NJ: Lawrence Erlbaum, 2006.

Parker, J., and E. Thorson, eds. *Health Communication in the New Media Landscape*. New York: Springer Publishing, 2009.

Scott, D.M. *The New Rules of Marketing and PR*. Hoboken, NJ: John Wiley & Sons, 2007.

On the Web

Andrew Keene talks about his book *The Cult of the Amateur*. http://www.youtube.com/watch?v=un5vTaUZvi4

Cision. "Rules of Engagement: Developing Effective Social Media Policies for Your Company & Employees." http://clients.marketingsavant.com/smbootcamp/docs/Guidelines%20-%20Policy/Cision_Developing_Social_Media_Policies.pdf

Day of the Longtail. http://www.youtube.com/watch?v=7xAA71Ssids

Evolution of Social Media (slide show). http://www.docstoc.com/docs/
  2900778/The-Evolution-of-Social-Media

Podcasting in Plain English. http://www.commoncraft.com/video/podcasting
  Privacy and Social Networks. http://www.youtube.com/watch?v=
  azIW1xjSTCo

RSS in Plain English. http://www.youtube.com/watch?v=0klgLsSxGsU

Social Bookmarking in Plain English. http://www.commoncraft.com/video/
  social-bookmarkingTwitter in Plain English. http://www.youtube.com/
  watch?v=ddO9idmax0o&feature=channel

What Is Social Media? (Common Craft video). http://www.youtube.com/
  watch?v=MpIOClX1jPE

Wikis in Plain English. http://www.youtube.com/watch?v=-dnL00TdmLY&
  feature=channel

LEVEL II

It All Begins at Home

Once you have taken into consideration why communication is important for a healthcare manager, and have examined and enhanced your own skills for the job, you have set the stage for looking beyond yourself to the specifics of the audiences with whom you are required to communicate.

On the second level, we will examine the audiences closest to home. You will find some interesting peculiarities about such audiences as employees, medical staff, and boards of trustees. Each of these groups and others like them have a vested interest in the successful achievement of your organization's overall mission and operational goals, just as you do. But they each view health care and the health-related organization from their own perspective.

The extent to which you understand the public relations (PR) function of your organization as something far beyond persuasion is a key part of your knowledge about communication. Even if your organization is a small one without a designated PR department, you still need to be concerned about the public relations aspects of your actions. The next few chapters will provide you with a foundation for understanding how to communicate with those audiences/publics closest to home.

7 Communicating In-house

Start with good people, lay out the rules, communicate with your employees, motivate them and reward them. If you do all these things effectively, you can't miss.
— Lee Iacocca

No matter how hard you might try, you can't avoid them. They are your employees, your organization's volunteers, your board members. They are the groups of people who are closest to home, and like you have a vested interest in your organization. How you communicate with them is fundamental to achieving the goals you have set. Strong internal communication is a key part of maintaining healthy relationships; poor communication can, in fact, be counterproductive, posing a threat to those relationships.[1]

> Research reveals that improving the communication of senior executives, especially the CEO, may be the most cost-effective way to improve employees' satisfaction with communication in their organizations.[2]

As we move through the early years of the twenty-first century, it is still hard to overstate the importance of internal communication. A study by Watson Wyatt Worldwide (2005/2006) found that organizations that excel in their internal communication tended to be more successful than those whose records were more dismal.

> The study found that companies with highly effective [internal] communication practices have a 19 per cent higher market premium, 57 per cent higher shareholder returns over five years, and a level of employee engagement that is 4.5 times higher than that of the competition.[3]

It is important, then, for you to examine your attitudes toward communicating with employees, your personal skills for doing so, and some of the communication practicalities you face on a daily basis.

Charity (and Other Things) Begins at Home

Consider the following scenario. Your hospital has been grappling with a budget deficit for the past two years. The employees are all aware of this, and the uncertainty about the future has already resulted in a considerable slide in morale, with all of its concomitant problems. As employees drive to work for the morning shift, a radio news report leaks information about possible layoffs at your institution today. The employees arrive at work to face the possibility of termination, and the fifty who actually receive pink slips are soon gone. Where does this leave the rest of your employees? More to the point, where does that leave you as a manager? How is your credibility? How do employees rate you in terms of your opinion of their importance? How important are employees?

Employees, medical staff, volunteers, and your board are crucial to your ability to accomplish anything at all. They are also your most important ambassadors to the outside world. So, not only is how you communicate with them important internally, but it also has a significant spin-off effect on the way you and your organization are perceived publicly.

Let's begin by examining your relationship (the outcome of your communication) with important internal groups. Consider your responses to the following questions.

- Do you generally feel comfortable when entering a meeting with each of the following groups?

  - your peers
  - medical staff
  - your employees
  - other health professionals
  - patients
  - your bosses

- Do you feel that the members of the above groups trust you? (What evidence do you have for your response?)
- Do you trust the members of the above groups?

The extent to which you have been able to nurture a positive relationship with each of these groups will affect your ability to achieve goals. How you communicate with them and why you do so are the key factors in these relationships.

The Healthcare Culture

Business schools like to talk a lot about *corporate culture*. Indeed, most healthcare managers who have formal education in administration will have studied the concept. Business schools, however, are notorious for neglecting to discuss in detail one of the most important contributing factors to the culture of the organization: communication. Both the general communication climate of the organization and the communication style of the senior managers are keys to deciphering the personality of the organization. If we are going to place internal communication into context, this is the best place to start.

Corporate Culture

We will begin by refreshing your memory about the concept of *corporate culture*. For many years, anthropologists were the only ones who seemed to be studying culture, defined in Webster's as "the sum total of the attainments and activities of any specific period, race or people, including their implements, handicrafts, agriculture, economics, music, art, religious beliefs, traditions, language and story."[4] So, we might use this as a template for defining organizational culture if we think of it as the history, mythology, beliefs, values, rituals, and jargon of any specific organization as they have evolved over time. By understanding an organization's cultural components, it is possible to begin to understand why the relationships exist as they are beyond any sense of logic. Relationships within organizations often defy logic. But why is it important to examine these relationships?

An organization's culture has often been referred to as the glue that holds it together. Strong cultures are characterized by high employee morale, a sense of shared vision, and high productivity. In health care, that translates into high-quality services delivered by highly competent, satisfied, loyal employees. As psychology professor Robert Taormina who has written extensively on the concept of organization socialization suggests: "... there should be some link between the employees and the organization, without which the overall relationship is likely to be a haphazard affair ..."[5] Communication is one of the most important keys to that relationship and the employees' fit into the culture.

Mission and Values

Many specific definitions of corporate culture exist: indeed, every writer seems to have developed his or her own definition. But several commonalities in the literature about corporate culture appear when we begin to examine the factors that serve to either enhance or detract from the strength of the culture. Obviously, a strong mission and core value system are important. We have already examined mission statements, but if you go back to the mission statement of your own organization, it is not enough that it sounds good and is well articulated. What is important here is how many of your employees actually know what the mission of your organization is, can relate it to others outside your organization, and actually buy into the values and philosophy.

One of the most striking examples of the strength a company gains from a shared value system was seen in the early 1980s when Johnson and Johnson faced what is now referred to by communication professionals as the "Tylenol Crisis." The company pulled their products off the shelves at an estimated cost to them of some $75 million, a major gamble in anyone's mind.

But how they came to the decision to do this is a striking example of a working philosophy doing its work.

Johnson and Johnson has a credo that was written in 1943 by the son of the company's founder. It starts off this way: "We believe our first responsibility is to the doctors, nurses, and patients, to mothers and all others who use our products and services."[6] The extent to which this philosophy has been internalized into the company's decision-making process is reflected in the words of Robert Kniffen, senior vice president of corporate relations, who was in the president's office at the time of the decision. He was quoted as saying: "It was not an instance where someone said, 'Let's consult the Credo and think through this problem,' but rather it was a way of looking at the world, at business and at a decision. The Credo structures the way you look at things."[7] A value system that is truly understood and embraced by an organization's employees is a powerful contribution to a strong culture – but it is not the only one.

History and Mythology

Another important factor in the development of a strong culture is a shared history and mythology. The history consists of the factual details of the organization's evolution, while the mythology develops from the stories that grow from that history.

Hospitals are especially fertile breeding grounds for mythology: the surgeon who throws instruments in the operating room (no one has actually seen it happen, but everyone has heard about it), or the patient who was found dead in the laundry cart (no one knows when it happened, but everyone knows about it). Each of these shared stories helps to glue the employees together.

Communication .

One of the most important aspects of what makes a culture strong is directly related to you, the manager. The communication style of the managers, and the communication climate that develops as a result, are keys to defining the organization's culture and, ultimately, the strength of the internal relationships.

A managerial communication style that fosters open, two-way communication within and among internal groups will have a significantly positive effect on the organizational climate. Employees and others who feel comfortable in both lauding as well as criticizing, and who recognize that someone will actually listen, are likely to have a stronger sense of loyalty, with a resultant increase in morale. Both the manager's verbal (oral and written) and nonverbal communication style will have an effect on the communication climate. It is also important to recognize that you may not be the best judge of your style.

Every year as I have guided students in conducting corporate culture assessments for clients, at least one manager (often a CEO) believes he or she has an "open-door" policy where employees feel comfortable coming in to discuss anything that concerns them. When employees are asked about this, they will say that one or more aspects of the manager's communication style makes them feel uncomfortable, and that they in fact don't believe that the manager has this "open-door" style. You often need an outsider to assess this for you, and you may not like what you hear. Listen anyway.

Service

Healthcare organizations are not unlike many other organizations in the factors that contribute to their culture. One thing that does, however, make it somewhat easier to foster the development of a strong culture is that many people who choose to work in this industry do so because of a desire to give service. This service-oriented mentality of healthcare workers can be used to its fullest advantage by managers. If your communication style is open and honest, and you share a service ethic with these workers, it may be easier to use this as the starting point for a shared vision. This shared vision in health care, communicated well to employees and other internal groups such as medical staff, can contribute to a healthy culture that fosters enhanced morale, increased productivity, and goal achievement.

Organizational "Climate"

Arguably even more important on a daily basis is the organizational climate. Whereas aspects of the culture are more nebulous and more difficult to measure, organizational climate can contribute to overall communication effectiveness and can actually be measured.

   The organizational climate consists of a variety of factors that include, among other things, leadership; organizational structure; accountability; behavioural standards; the reward system; trust; and perhaps most important, communication.[8] These dimensions of the work environment all contribute to the effectiveness of the communication and the subsequent strength of the relationships forged.

Your Internal Audience

The types of people who work in health-related organizations today have changed. Indeed, this is a reflection of the changes in the overall workforce since the 1950s. Generally, the work force in North America now is more highly educated; more cynical; more insecure; and, as a result, more territorial. They are children of the television era and now of interconnected, worldwide computer technology. They take less at face value and are much more difficult to mislead. They have access to social media networks that provide more feedback than ever before considered possible. There are more women (especially in healthcare delivery), and there is a more diverse multicultural representation.

All of these factors have conspired to alter the way managers must think about the way they communicate. Even the use of nonsexist, inclusive language, an unknown issue just a generation ago, is an important communication result of these changes.

If we examine the changes in the nursing profession over the past half century for example, we can see a striking illustration of just such a phenomenon. In 1960, American nurse Peggy Nuttal wrote a book titled *Nursing as a Career*[9] to provide potential nurses with information on what to expect in a career as a nurse. She begins her discussion of nursing by describing the personal characteristics that make for a suitable nursing candidate. Her first characteristic is that she [sic] should like people. Later she lists other favoured characteristics such as a sense of humour, reliability, being good with your hands, and being fit. These are all probably good ideas (for anyone in a health profession) even today, but it is more likely that the American and Canadian Nurses' associations might suggest that she or he should be bright, articulate, assertive, empathetic, and politically aware. This is a far cry from how Florence Nightingale saw nurses in 1881 when she suggested that a good nurse was a good woman who demonstrated a higher nature that included quietness, gentleness, patience, and endurance.

The reality is that when you look at the nurses sitting across from you at the union bargaining table, patience may or may not be one of the virtues you encounter, but quietness and gentleness are not likely to be in great abundance. You need to communicate with these women and men differently than your predecessors did. Knowing your audience is half the battle.

This concept is probably best illustrated when considering your communication with physicians. Professional socialization of physicians is quite different from that of administrative personnel, thus the way they see the world is different than you might see it resulting in differing views on communication. According to Kenneth Cohn, a surgeon who also consults widely on the topic of physician-hospital relations and healthcare communication, "Physicians are like university professors, whose primary allegiance is to their subject matter (first), colleagues (second), and workplace (a distant third)."[10] Writing in the *Journal of Healthcare Management*, he further suggests that there are three main areas in which physicians and hospitals differ in their thinking and their vocabulary. They are *time frame* (time frames are shortened, i.e., "'now' to a physician means without delay, whereas to an administrator, it may mean the next budget cycle"[11]); *team orientation* (physicians think in terms of "individual contributions" whereas administrators and managers think in terms of interdependence); and *control* (physicians control people and processes rather than the administrative conception of control of assets of other types[12]). Clearly being able to communicate requires a deep understanding of the mindset *and* vocabulary of the other party.

Pressures

Pressures on the healthcare systems – regardless of their public or private nature – have changed the outlook of many health professionals with whom you will communicate. These pressures, such as litigation, insurance issues, and increasing consumer demands, have made many healthcare workers, particularly physicians, wary of anything that smacks of bureaucracy. As a healthcare manager at any level, you represent this. Communicating with wary groups of health professionals requires an empathetic attitude and skills that enable you to tailor your message and approach to an understanding of where they are coming from.

Technology

Another factor that you must consider in your communication with health professionals is the effect that increasing technology has had on their ranks. As medical technology has advanced over the past half century, so too have the numbers of specialized allied health professions required to work with these new technologies. For example, before the advent of ultrasonography, there were no sonography technicians; before open-heart surgery and dialysis, there were no perfusionists. Add to this the move to enhance the responsibilities of nurses with some procedures previously performed only by doctors, and you blur the lines of responsibility and increase the potential for turf wars. It is within this climate that you as a manager must communicate with other health professionals.

The other aspect of technology that has been brought to bear on internal communication is the advent of social media. No longer are your employees and other internal groups consigned to be receivers of information providing feedback only when asked. They are able not only to provide feedback whenever they choose by posting their impressions online; they are also content creators. This adds an uncontrollable element to the internal communication mix that needs to be addressed in communication and employee policy and procedures. (See our discussion in chapter 6.)

Volunteers

Volunteers are another group that a healthcare manager needs to communicate with on a regular basis. Many healthcare organizations rely on volunteers in working toward the organization's goal. In smaller, nonprofit organizations volunteers may be the lifeblood without which you cannot survive. For other, larger institutions, volunteers may have a more specific role, such as in fund-raising. Whatever role they play in your own organization, they are an important part of the internal public, but they are not the same as paid employees. They need at all times to feel rewarded in other ways than monetary – and this morale boosting should colour the tone of all communication that management has with volunteers. This should be your communication theme.

Your Board

One of the most important internal audiences that you have is your board. If you are, or at some point in your career will be, at a senior level in healthcare administration, then communicating with your board is an important issue. We will discuss this in detail in an upcoming chapter.

Knowing as much as you can about your audience allows you to develop a communication style that is more likely to be accepted by that audience. Your messages, channels, and tone will be audience specific.

Communicating Internally

Once you have acknowledged that you are communicating on a daily basis with diverse internal audiences (who should share a common vision), you need to examine the purpose of this communication and the approaches you will use.

As we have discussed previously, there are essentially only two general categories of communication. You are either engaged in one-way communication where the messages originate with you and the process is over when the message has been received by the audience, or two-way communication wherein you consider and act on feedback from your audience in response to your first communication.

An overall style categorized by one-way communication is considered to be a closed approach. Overuse of one-way communication by managers contributes to a weak culture and a morale-dampening internal climate with all their concomitant negative consequences. One-way techniques, used in conjunction with other approaches (where your employees and other staff already recognize that they have other opportunities for feedback), are sometimes the most efficient ways to convey information. You provide the information that the internal group needs. Indeed, access to online communities has made the notion of one-way communication rather quaint in any case.

There are, however, many reasons why you communicate with internal groups, and most of them require two-way methods. You should be thinking constantly about how to open a dialogue and deal with the feedback that is to come. In other words, you should be thinking about engaging with your internal publics.

Persuasion is sometimes a goal in your communication. You may need to have internal groups on-side for changes that are coming. You may need to persuade them to management's point of view.

Often, the purpose of your communication will be to build morale. In fact, you might want to consider that you are either contributing to enhanced morale or detracting from it every time you communicate. Examine your memos, your message in the newsletter, your e-mail correspondence, and your demeanour at meetings and presentations. Do they all have a positive component for internal groups? If not, you will need to change the tone of your messages. It is always possible to enhance morale, even when conveying negative news, if you consider your tone, the subliminal message underlying your words, and your presentation. And never forget that every time you walk down a hall, employees will draw conclusions from your nonverbal behaviour. You are on display at all times.

Communicating with Patients

Whether you refer to those served by your organization as patients (hospitals), clients (clinics), or residents (long-term care), these people constitute an important internal group while they are receiving services, and even after the service is finished. Managers in health-related organizations need to feel comfortable communicating with these groups for a variety of reasons.

The most important reason is that patients who perceive that they have been listened to are happier patients. A fair amount of research supports the contention that patients who believe they have a positive relationship with their healthcare providers are less likely to take legal action against an individual or institution. It is important to provide high-quality, competent services, but the communication environment and the relationships that develop as a result are also vital.

Although the obvious health benefits of calm, satisfied patients seems to be an important enough reason to ensure that communication with patients is high quality, avoiding litigation is one that cannot be ignored either.

Depending upon your administrative level, you will have varying numbers of direct contacts with patients. As a senior administrator, you may hear from patients and their families only when there is either a problem or when they want to pay your organization a compliment. At lower levels, you may have day-to-day, face-to-face contact. Your level will determine the amount and method of communication, but the importance is the same at all levels.

If you have not already instituted them, you should consider conducting patient/client satisfaction surveys from time to time, ensuring that a large portion of the survey deals with the perceived communication competence of the organization. Online methods have made it much easier for even small healthcare organizations to do this. Simple, widely available online software such as Survey Monkey (www.surveymonkey.com) and Fluidsurveys (www.fluidsurveys.com) can make the process very easy as long as you have some assistance in the development of useful, comprehensible questions.

Hospital Jargon: Good or Bad?

Several different kinds of jargon colour the verbal communication in healthcare institutions. First, there is the medical terminology. Although it is a necessary part of the communication between health professionals, such terminology can interfere with accurate message receipt by patients and their families. Health professionals at the individual level must learn to deal with this, ensuring that excessive medical terminology doesn't creep into their communication with patients or clients without explanation. Then there are all the acronyms and abbreviations that make their way into verbal and written communication. Ensuring that your communication with patients is not peppered with them can be a challenge.

There is also what I like to call secret medical "in-talk." If you spend any time around house staff (in teaching hospitals in particular), you hear this jargon. It is not always complimentary, but it is part of the hospital culture. Usually, health professionals use these expressions when talking to one another, and they are generally quite careful not to use this terminology around patients. In fact, American folklore researchers believe that sometimes these expressions are used by health professionals to actively conceal information from patients[13] (like the parent who spells something out in front of a young child).

The most widely recognized example of this is the term "gomer" (or more accurately GOMER). If you are familiar with Samuel Shem's irreverent medical novel *The House of God*,[14] you may recognize it. The term is usually used to refer to elderly, male patients, often chronically alcoholic, who arrive in the emergency room on a rather regular basis. But it has a number of interpretations, one of which is that it stands for "get out of my emergency room." Ask any emergency room physician if he or she has heard it.

Another acronym that has gained popularity over the years is FLK. It stands specifically for "funny looking kid" and is used to refer quickly to a child that at first glance doesn't look quite right, but there hasn't yet been time for a diagnosis. It allows for the examining health professional to flag the unusual look of the child, often a newborn, so that time can be taken later to assess for problems. It is not meant for the patient. In fact, a news story in Canada reported that a mother was offended when she happened to see this written about her child, threatening to sue for defamation (it turned out that the child did, indeed, have a medical problem). There have been no further developments on this case in the media, but it points to an important issue.

Healthcare organizations have their own jargon for communication with one another, but the health workers who use these terms need to be careful about how and when they use them. They are never appropriate messages to convey to patients. As a manager, it is your responsibility to be a communication role model by encouraging your staff to speak and communicate appropriately, especially around patients.

The Hospital Grapevine

Is it a real communication method? You bet it is, and one that shouldn't be ignored. Most organizations, unless they are one-person operations, have a grapevine of some sort or another. Many public relations practitioners and scholars consider the grapevine to be one of the most powerful means of communication within an organization.

When a rumour gains steam, it is almost impossible to stop, and you will almost never figure out who started it. It has been suggested that the attractiveness of the grapevine is a function of the fact that it is so heady. The *truth* and *facts* are much duller. In the recent past we have had to deal with the accelerated pace of the grapevine as a result of e-mails: now we have to consider other forms of online communication as well. If e-mail made the grapevine lightning fast, then social media have conspired to put it into the equivalent of a particle accelerator. Not only can employees send gossip and rumours to one another as individuals through the grapevine, they can (and do) post such musings on their Facebook sites, chat rooms, forums, YouTube, personal blogs, and so on. All of these are grapevine vehicles with incredible reach.

According to business professor Jitendra M. Mishra, "Bosses who choose not to pay attention to the grapevine have 50% less credible information than those who do."[15] So, how do you deal with the grapevine in these days of the Web-vine? First, stay tuned in to it. The organizational grapevine is a fact of life and can also be an effective means of communicating information. Second, be prepared to correct any misconstrued information before it causes a problem within the ranks of your employees, volunteers, medical staff, and board. The grapevine is a wide-spreading entity and can even reach out and touch the community and the media. Third, ensure that your institution has well-considered, regularly updated policies on employee use of social media, as we have discussed previously. One plank of your policy that you might consider is limiting the extent to which employees are permitted to identify their place of employment in personal communication of this kind.

There are two important grapevine truths to remember:

- The grapevine is always going to be there; however,
- Employees still prefer to receive information from official sources.

Credibility versus Full Disclosure

Although this issue of credibility is not specific to internal communication, it is a particularly important issue at this juncture. Clearly, truth in managerial communication is key to the manager's credibility, and is a value to be pursued. There is, however, another perspective that needs consideration. That comes from answering the questions: How much disclosure is enough to be truthful? How much is too much?

Open communication doesn't necessarily mean telling everything. Public relations consultant Diana Morris reports on a situation with one of her clients, a revered and prosperous community hospital that was dealing with merger offers one after another by refusing all of them. From a communication perspective, the hospital administration prided itself in openness and frankness, telling everything about the offers and their adamant refusal to merge.

Finally, pressures on hospitals being what they were in the 1990s, they finally accepted one of the offers and merged with another hospital. The hospital brought in a communications consultant when they perceived that there may have been problems with the way their communication was handled. The consultant discovered that employees were very negative. They had lost all faith in the credibility of management communication because they had been told so much about how the hospital would not merge, but then it turned out differently. One employee put it this way: "Why do they always contradict themselves? As far as I am concerned, communication at this hospital has no credibility."[16]

This is a striking case in support of the notion that, despite all good intentions for honesty and openness in communication, telling employees everything is unnecessary and can even be damaging. This means that great care and judgment must be exercised in making these decisions. What to tell, what not to tell, how much to tell, and when, are not in opposition to honesty.

Chapter 7 Key Points

1. Employees prefer important information to come directly from their supervisors in face-to-face encounters.
2. Your relationships with key internal groups such as employees, medical staff, volunteers, and your board are significantly affected by your ability to communicate with them.
3. The culture or climate of the organization is significantly affected by managerial communication style.
4. A healthcare organization with a weak culture is more likely to have difficulty meeting its goals.
5. You may not be the best judge of how your communication style is perceived by employees.
6. Internal audiences have changed in significant ways over the past fifty' years, and your understanding of these characteristics is crucial to your ability to communicate.
7. In every communication encounter you have with internal groups or individuals, you are either contributing to or detracting from morale.
8. Patients or clients in healthcare institutions are less likely to take legal action against organizations and/or individuals who they believe have communicated well with them.
9. Never ignore the hospital grapevine.
10. Honesty in internal communication is not synonymous with full disclosure.

For Your Bookshelf

Holz, Shel. *Corporate Conversations: A Guide to Crafting Effective and Appropriate Internal Communication*. New York: American Management Association, 2004.

LeMenager, Jack. *Inside the Organization: Perspectives on Employee Communication*. Winchester, MS: Fells Publishing, 2011.

Smith, Lynn, and Pamela Mounter. *Effective Internal Communication*. 2nd ed. London: Kogan-Page, 2008.

On the Web

Interpretive Models of Employee Engagement. http://www.scotland.gov.uk/
    Publications/2007/05/09111348/5
Tips for the Workplace: The Role of Communication. http://www.mphwa.org/
    tipsfortheworkplace.htm

8 Communicating Strategically with Your Board

Three people were at work on a construction site. All were doing the same job, but when each was asked what the job was, the answers varied. "Breaking rocks," the first replied. "Earning my living," the second said. "Helping to build a cathedral," said the third.

— Peter Schultz

We all see things from our own point of view. Boards, however, often seem to have more than one perspective from which to interpret the world.

If you think about it, your board is really a hybrid of your internal and external communities; although when it comes to having their "say" on organizational matters, they are firmly entrenched (at least in their minds) insiders. Perhaps you see them differently. The following diagram provides a visual illustration of where the interfaces are and where the pressures on the relationship originate. Notice that pressures on the relationships can originate from either inside or outside the organization.

The fragility of the relationship between board and management can stem from the simple truth that you are on the inside every day, and they are not. Therein rests both their strength and their weakness.

Being on the outside looking in provides an oft-needed objective eye. When you are so close that you can't see the forest for the trees, it can help to have strong rapport with a group one step removed. Further, this external view provides important input that may reflect where their other foot is planted – namely, the external community. That external input coming from a group that has a vested interest in what you are doing is valuable.

Figure 8.1 Your Organization/Your Board/Your Community

On the other hand, as many healthcare managers have learned from hard experience, boards sometimes can't quite grasp the rhyme and reason of what are now the realities of today's healthcare industry. In health care, perhaps more than in any other industry, self-identification can cloud the reasoning of even the most level-headed board member. The emotion and value-laden characteristics of health care sometimes make that highly regarded objectivity a fleeting commodity.

Therefore, the relationship between administration and board, fuelled as it is by communication processes, can be a challenging one. However, being strategic about communication with your board can go a long way toward building a mutually beneficial relationship and your own credibility.

If you are a front-line or middle manager, your direct communication with your healthcare institution's board may be almost nil. That does not mean that you should ignore the nuances of how the channels of communication shape decisions that will ultimately affect you both as an employee and as a manager.

The Power of Your Board

"Most affairs of American life are controlled or influenced by boards."[1] This is the opening line in Cyril O. Houle's book *Governing Boards*, and a scary one at that. Houle goes on to give us chapter and verse about the kinds of groups who sit around "boardrooms" (they are everywhere, aren't they?) and make decisions that affect our lives. He lists churches; governments; private corporations; educational institutions; professional organizations; trade unions; not-for-profits; and, of course, healthcare organizations, to name a few.

Could your organization accomplish its goals without a board? Think very carefully about your answer. Your positive or negative response is likely to be directly correlated to the quality of your own personal relationship with your board, or the preconceived notions you hold if you are currently at a level in the hierarchy where you do not yet have any direct interaction with your board. Whether you believe that they are effective or not, they do have a degree of power that is a reflection of the trust (hence the term *trustees*) that your community has in your board's role in protecting their interests. A wise administrator respects that public trust and recognizes the image power that a board has. This alone makes strategic communication with your board vital – not for the purpose of controlling them, but for developing a rapport with them.

Communicating with a Purpose

It may seem self-evident why high-level managers and executives need to communicate with their boards. But if you consider this *just another part of your managerial duties* when you are at that level, you have missed the point of recognizing the importance of *strategic* communication. There should never be an encounter between you or your managers and your board that is not purposeful and well considered.

Inform

The first strategic purpose of communication with your board is a result of their view of themselves as insiders. They have informational needs. Thus, your goal is to inform. What you inform them about, to what extent, and when are strategic considerations.

Board members need information about

- background on issues that they will consider as part of their role as board members,
- actions taken by administration that are likely to be made known publicly,
- any new or unusual occurrences that are being made public through the media whether traditional or new media.

Essentially, your board members need enough information to do their jobs and to feel that they are important insiders. In addition to this, because they are important external ambassadors of your organization, they need to be "kept in the loop" about issues that are or will be of a public nature. There is nothing more irritating for a board member than to hear about an organization's activities in the news or from a neighbour. If you want to incite them to riot, just treat them with less consideration than you do your employees.

Obviously, your opinion about how much information they need to do their jobs may differ from their opinions about how much information they need. In addition, there are likely to be differing perspectives on this issue from one board member to another. This is why a good personal relationship with the board chair can be helpful for health-care managers at the top of the organizational hierarchy. Your own interpersonal skills are called into play in the development of your relationship.

A good board chair who understands administration's point of view (although he or she might not always agree with it) can be a formidable ally in your quest to woo your board. Cultivating this interpersonal relationship can be a key element in your ability to communicate your messages effectively to them.

Persuade

The second important purpose for communication with your board is to persuade them about issues for which, from your perspective at least, you need their support. One of the most important aspects of persuasion when dealing with your board is to ensure that you tailor your message specifically to this audience. It will not be effective enough to simply use the same approach that you use for this issue with clients and the community, or even your employees for that matter. You need to think very carefully about packaging the persuasive message for your board. This may mean thinking about each individual's perspective as you prepare for any presentation of a persuasive nature.

Packaging Your Communication

Just as important as purpose and message when communicating with your board, so too are when and how you do it.

When

The first rule of when to communicate with your board is to do it regularly. And this does not mean only at scheduled board meetings. You need a vehicle for direct communication between the highest levels of administration in your organization and all board members between board meetings. If your organization is of any size at all, you need to put this in writing.

As the CEO, you'll need to develop a communication vehicle whose objectives are to

- nurture your relationship with each board member,
- inform them of information in a timely fashion, and
- cultivate within them a feeling of belonging to your organization.

How

From these objectives come the content and the vehicle for sharing the information. Consider each of these objectives to ensure that any material you send achieves each one, every time. Following are some suggestions for the kind of materials that would help to move you toward your goals:

- a monthly message from the CEO and/or other managers: the vehicle you choose depends on your board whose media preferences should be well known to you,
- an intranet that is updated regularly,
- a media monitor with explanatory notes as necessary,
- a calendar of internal events as well as external events that your organization may be participating in.

There was a time when debates on the efficacy of electronic distribution raged. In general, those debates are over: electronic distribution is expected and usually preferred by most people these days. That being said, there may be reasons to include print publications in your communication repertoire. Knowing your board members and their preferences can help to guide your decision on the most appropriate vehicles for informational and persuasive communication approaches.

Board – administration communication can often be a special challenge for healthcare managers. If you share a vision and a set of core

Figure 8.2 Characteristics of Effective Board Communication

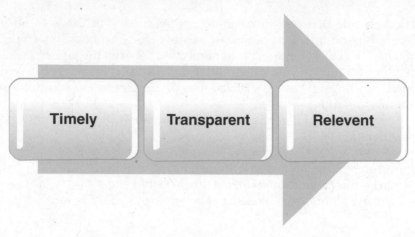

values, however, communication will at least have a common ground from which to start. After that it is up to you.

Your personal skills in communication are essential to both you and your organization.

As one blogger[2] suggests, make your board communication timely, transparent, and relevant.

Chapter 8 Key Points

1. The main goal of strategic communication with your board is to enhance your rapport and the relationship that emanates from it.
2. The goal of communication with your board is not to control them.
3. Two important objectives for communication encounters with board members are to inform and to persuade.
4. The first rule of management–board communication is to do it regularly.
5. The second rule of management–board communication is to have a specific vehicle for doing it.
6. Your own personal skills in interpersonal and written communication as well as your ability to make presentations are key to successful management–board communication.

For Your Bookshelf

Joshi, Maulik, and Bernard Horak. *Healthcare Transformation: A Guide for the Hospital Board Member.* Boca Raton, FL: Taylor & Francis, 2009.

On the Web

"Five Ways to Improve Internal Communications at Your Non-profit." https://charityvillage.com/Content.aspx?topic=five_ways_to_improve_internal_communications_at_your_nonprofit
"7 Strategies for More Productive Non-Profit Board Meetings." http://www.thefundraisingauthority.com/strategy-and-planning/more-productive-board-meetings/

9 Working with PR and Corporate Communications

Alone we can do so little; together we can do so much.

– Helen Keller

"Bring in the PR people!"

It seems like a familiar refrain. When have you heard those infamous words? Does it happen when things are going smoothly? Or have you more frequently heard them when something within your organization has gone wrong or is about to go wrong? Strikes, sexual harassment charges, lawsuits, medical malpractice – these are just a few of the unpleasant situations that can plague a healthcare manager and send you rushing to the PR people before the media are on your doorstep.

If you are working within a large enough organizational structure, you are probably fortunate to have a public relations staff. But do you really use them to their fullest advantage? Do you even know what they are capable of doing for your organization? One of the most important parts of healthcare communication on a macro level (beyond you as the individual communicator) is the public relations function of your department or organization. If you are part of a small organization that does not have the luxury of such specialized communication staff, then you are it.

In this chapter we will examine what modern public relations practice can be expected to accomplish and look at the difference between PR and marketing, as well as the similarities between the skills required for PR and fund-raising. In the end, you should be able to assess the public relations function in your organization or department and use their expertise to your best advantage.

Who "They" Are and What "They" Do

It would be derelict of anyone writing about healthcare communication to neglect a specific discussion of healthcare public relations. In general terms, modern public relations is the strategic application of communications tools and techniques to help organizations develop and maintain relationships. Public relations requires practitioners who have managerial and technical skills, creativity, integrity, and flexibility. Indeed, most modern PR people consider public relations to be a managerial function – and broadly speaking, it is in the best interests of an organization to consider public relations in this context. There are, however, both managerial and technical levels to public relations, and it is useful for other managers to understand these two levels.

Relationships

Before we can differentiate between these two levels, it is important for healthcare managers to understand something about relationships. We have discussed them in specific situations up to this point, but let's take a step back for a moment to consider their broader context.

The two most important aspects of an organization's relationships – both internal and external – are as follows:

• The development and nurturing of strong, long-term relationships with a variety of publics is key to any organization's image and identity, public goodwill, and ultimate ability to achieve its mission.
• Communication with these publics, whether that communication is intentional, unintentional, proactive, or reactive is what builds those relationships.

Your own communication skills as a manager contribute in a large way to the development of those relationships, whether at the departmental or organizational level.

Consider a manager at the lower levels of a hospital hierarchy. This manager likely has direct contact with patients and thus can have considerable effect on the development of that hospital's external image. A manager at this level whose communication skills are well honed can leave a very positive image of that organization with patients or clients who are likely to talk about the organization positively to outsiders. This helps to build positive relationships with the community.

A CEO can also have the same kind of effects on a higher level of the hierarchy. Make no mistake, however. Regardless of your managerial level in a health-related organization, your own skills and strategic understanding of communication will have effects, intended or not, on the relationships that both you and your organization build with a variety of publics.

PR Technicians

Public relations practitioners see themselves in two ways. First are the PR technicians. These individuals are trained in the development of communication tools and techniques that can be applied to the implementation of a plan that they may or may not have been involved in developing. For example, a PR technician writes news releases and designs and writes newsletters, annual reports, brochures, promotional video scripts, updates the Twitter feed and Facebook presence, contributes to Web site maintenance. In short, the technician carries out many of the activities that have been planned by the communication management team of the organization.

PR Managers

Public relations managers – in addition to the technical work that may be required of them from time to time – also develop the strategic communication plan for the organization and manage the human and other resource aspects of the implementation of the plan. In the real world of small public relations departments, these people may be one and the same, although some PR technicians are better equipped than others to carry out the managerial aspects of a higher-level position. For example, someone trained in journalism is likely to make a very good PR technician, but unless that individual's education is supplemented by a serious dose of mentoring in public relations planning, he or she will probably lack the strategic thinking required to be a PR manager.

What PR Offers

What then, specifically, does the public relations function have to offer healthcare organizations? It can do some or all of the following:

- Assist the organization in the development of a healthy public image so that even during times of crisis, the organization is likely to get a fair hearing.
- Work with the management of the organization to develop strategies for handling many kinds of potential problems.
- Help prepare for media encounters and assist you with your writing/editing/speaking engagements.
- Support the marketing of your services (including conferences and events) if that is part of what you require (more about the marketing function later).
- Conduct community and other stakeholder engagement.
- Provide environmental scanning and issues management advice.
- Act as key contact or spokesperson for the organization with community agencies and the media.

Many people outside the public relations field see public relations as synonymous with publicity. Although generating publicity is a part of the one-way communication function that any good public relations person can do well, it is only a very small part. Generating publicity is often a good thing; however, not all publicity is positive for the organization. Thus, even potentially publicity-generating activities must be carefully considered within an overall plan for managing the organization's relationships.

With all this emphasis on public relations as a management function, it should be clear to any healthcare manager that today's public relations people are better used as fire preventers than firefighters. In other words, don't wait until there is a crisis before bringing in the PR people.

Public Relations or Marketing?

Marketing has become a fact of life for most organizations involved in health care, whether they like it or not. By definition, marketing means selling a service or product to a customer, the hallmark of which is an exchange of some sort, usually money, for the purchase of the goods or service. As public relations authors Scott Cutlip, Allen Center, and Glen Broom say, "The hospital industry is increasingly embroiled in public policy debates and aggressively pursuing patients."[1] Clearly, pursuing patients is more of a focus in a private healthcare system or organization, but the marketing activities required can also prove effective in public and not-for-profit enterprises in terms of their contribution to reputation and relationship building. Isn't public relations, then, just a part of the marketing plan? Clearly not. But they work beautifully together.

We have already established that public relations is responsible for the nurturing of long-term relationships with a variety of publics, all of whose goodwill is important to the successful achievement of the healthcare organization's mission. This is not the same as marketing, but the two are, indeed, related.

Traditionally, marketing and public relations used to be differentiated by the simple exhortation that marketing sells goods and services, while public relation sells the organization and its image. This definition is far too simplistic, and it fails to recognize that modern public relations practice often finds itself in the uncomfortable position of having to advise management that they need to be honest about their shortcomings – hardly what one would term "selling" the organization – to fulfil their obligation to the greater good.

Another way of differentiating between PR and marketing has been to indicate that marketers use advertising (paid, controlled media), while PR uses publicity (free, uncontrolled media). This is certainly no longer true since marketers have recognized the marketing value of some of these public relations techniques, and PR has increasingly turned to paid advertising to control the message. This is especially true in the digital age where *it is no longer possible to do so any other way*.

The best way to think about the differences between these two external communications functions is to consider the kind of relationship that is the objective of each. Marketers seek to develop a relationship with current and potential customers/clients/patients so that the services offered by that particular organization are selected by the customer/client/patient when the need to purchase arises. Thus, this short-term, in-the-moment relationship is an important one. Eventually, the marketers might be interested in maintenance of these customers, but when you come right down to it, the relationship at that moment of decision is all important.

The aim of a public relations strategy overall, on the other hand, is to develop and nurture long-term relationships with a variety of publics so that the organization's positive reputation allows it to accomplish a variety of objectives, not just selling their services. For example, positive public relations is widely believed to provide for the greater likelihood of fair coverage by media, for community support in ventures such as expansion, for employee buy-in of mergers and acquisitions, for attracting high-quality medical and allied health staff, for positive relationships with funders, and for decreasing the likelihood of litigation. Positive public relations outcomes also support the marketing effort of the organization by creating a climate of goodwill that allows potential customers/clients/patients to emerge from the community. Marketing can then take over in that area.

Marketing of healthcare services, however, differs in several important ways from the marketing of other goods and services. Most healthcare executives are well aware of these differences.

- The individual (or group) actually paying for the services is often not the person selecting the service provider (i.e., insurance companies have limited control over selection and cost decisions).
- The nature and location of that service are generally not controlled by the person receiving the service (i.e., physicians make the recommendations).
- Healthcare services are often unpleasant for the purchaser.[2]

Thus, long-term relationships with physicians and insurers are just as important as the long-term relationships with clients.

Healthcare organizations today need both public relations and marketing to function optimally. They work together, but conceptually, they are two different communication functions.

Public Relations and Fund-raising

There is a natural relationship between public relations and fund-raising. For nonprofit healthcare organizations, fund-raising is often crucial to their operation, and what is fund-raising if not a communication activity? How do these two fall together?

In many smaller organizations, public relations and development are not only the same department, but often use the skills and services of the same individuals. Obviously, an organization cannot raise funds successfully if it has a poor public image. Thus, the relationships that public relations activities build are fundamental to fund-raising. Once that image is nurtured, then a fund-raising case needs to be communicated to the targeted potential donors. Public relations' communication expertise must be utilized in this exercise as well. To summarize:

Public relations representatives participate directly in fund-raising by organizing and conducting solicitation programs, or they serve as consultants to specialized development departments of their organizations. Organizations often employ professional firms to conduct their campaigns on a fee basis. In that case, the organization's public relations representatives usually have a liaison function.[3]

It would be impossible to conduct a fund-raising campaign of any sort without communicating your messages skilfully to your target donors. Thus, for a nonprofit organization, formal public relations expertise is crucial.

If You Don't Have a PR Staff

If you are a manager in a small organization that does not have the luxury of professional communicators on staff, then you are "it." Your best strategy is to ferret out as many communications and public relations professionals in your community as you can and beg them to help you set up a volunteer PR committee, staffed with people who possess the required expertise. This group can become the core of experts that you use to develop a plan for public relations and to train you and your staff. The training should consist of helping everyone in your organization to understand the importance of public relations and its relationship to the success of your organization. The training should also help managers to hone their communication skills.

In addition to these functions, your volunteer public relations consultants can also provide you with considerable technical expertise as you develop and use specific tools such as news releases, brochures, annual reports, and media kits, and develop your organization's social media strategy.

Take advantage of every opportunity you have to attend professional development seminars presented by the organizations to which communicators belong. Some Web sites listed at the end of this chapter can guide you to your local chapters.

It is extremely important for managers in healthcare organizations, whether they have professional public relations help or not, to familiarize themselves with the roles and functions of a public relations staff. To neglect this is to neglect an important part of your overall strategy for accomplishing your organizational goals.

Using Outside PR Consultants

In these times of increasing outsourcing, many high-ranking executives have determined that it is best to outsource their public relations and communication activities. However, because healthcare organizations have some very specific needs, hiring outside help for all PR activities is not always the best choice.

Health care requires individuals with certain sensitivities to issues such as client confidentiality and an appreciation that the services provided by that organization are frequently unpleasant for those clients. Having in-house staff allows a healthcare organization to select communicators with the personal philosophies that are consistent with the mission of the organization. In addition, from the perspective of other health professionals within the organization, someone from the outside is likely to be viewed with some suspicion. Thus, whenever financially feasible, it is always in the best interests of a healthcare organization to have its own public relations staff. There are, however, times when even an organization with a well-staffed PR function must, or at least should, hire outside consultants.

Here are several different scenarios where an outside public relations consultant would be beneficial and even preferable to internal staff:

- When you have specific communication activities that need to be accomplished and insufficient staff. For example, your staff might be completely capable of organizing a large event such as an open house or a fund-raising dinner, but they may not have the human resources to do so.
- When the communications task is outside the area of your internal staff's expertise. If you are merging with another healthcare institution, it may be preferable to hire an outside public relations consultant who has been through such a situation with other organizations. They are more likely to be able to anticipate public relations problems (especially ones with your internal groups) before they arise.
- When you need to assess the quality of your current public relations programming. Part of a high-quality public relations function is the necessity for evaluation of outcomes. Hiring an outside consultant every three to five years to conduct a public relations audit is a very wise idea. While any competent PR practitioner can audit his or her own department's function, this person can't be relied upon for

objectivity. An outside perspective can be extremely valuable as you move toward new goals.

Whereas this is not the place for a detailed discussion of how to hire a public relations consultant, there are some tips that can be helpful. Keep in mind that there are similarities in hiring any kind of outside consultant, and your past experience in hiring others is applicable in this situation. The following are some questions that may assist you in beginning your search.

- *What services do they offer?*

  - media relations and/or media training
  - government relations
  - lobbying
  - employee relations
  - client relations
  - board relations
  - donor relations
  - issues management
  - crisis communication management
  - community relations
  - print media development
  - broadcast media development
  - social media strategy development
  - social media policy development

- *What size of organization have they worked with in the past?* One size does not fit all. If you are part of a small, long-term care facility, their experience with large, tertiary care hospitals may not provide them with the kind of background that you need.
- *What types of organizations have they worked with in the past?* A public relations consultant who has never worked with a healthcare organization is not a good fit for you. There would be a steep learning curve for a consultant who is not familiar with the external and internal environments of health care. In addition, if you are a nonprofit organization, does the consultant have experience with nonprofits?
- *Where are they physically located?* Do they have a geographic presence in your community? If they don't, you need to assess the amount and kind of personal, face-to-face contact that will be necessary for

you and to meet the expectations of your staff. If you have a choice to use local consultants or ones from afar, you are usually better to use local.

- *Can they provide you with a list of past clients*? If you see any personal contacts on their list, call those first. Listen to what your contacts are saying and what they are not saying. If you don't see any contacts, look to other healthcare leaders who are members of one of the professional organizations to which you belong. Failing that, cold call those who seem to represent similar kinds of organizations to your own.

Finally, there is one last question that you need to ask, and you need to do your due diligence to elicit the answer:

- *What is their online presence like*? This requires some research into their Web site, their Twitter feed, their Facebook presence, their LinkedIn activity, their blogs, and any other social media activity in which they participate. Keep in mind that public relations professionals have been among the early adopters of social media tools and tactics, and you can glean a lot of information, especially as regards "fit" with your organizational culture from the material you find online.

Public relations consultants can provide much-needed expertise to individual healthcare executives and their organizations. They can even be cost effective. Public relations in health care, however, is a necessary internal requirement.

Your PR Function: How Does It Measure Up?

A well-functioning public relations department, even if it consists of only one person, needs to be assessed from time to time. Knowing the questions to ask makes this assessment much easier. Here are the questions that you need to ask regularly.

1. Is your public relations function headed by a competent, well-educated PR professional?
2. Is your PR staff at the boardroom table?
3. Are they doing environmental scanning (i.e., gathering data about the external environment)?
4. Do you receive regular reports of the results of this scanning?

5. Do you approve an operational PR plan at least annually?
6. Do they have a good grasp of health care and how it is organized?
7. Do you receive a media monitoring report each month?
8. Are they up to date on all the newest social media issues and tools?
9. Are your policies for clearance (e.g., who has to approve media releases, etc.) clear, efficient, and used at all times?
10. Does your PR staff evaluate its activities on a regular basis?

If you answered no to any of these questions, then you have a problem area within your PR function. You need to carefully examine how you are using your staff and consider how to fix the problems.

Chapter 9 Key Points

1. Modern public relations practice is the strategic application of communication tools and techniques to help organizations develop and manage their relationships with important internal and external groups.
2. Public relations is loosely divided by its technical and managerial functions – and healthcare organizations need both.
3. Generating publicity (a good example of one-way communication) is only a very small part of modern public relations.
4. Public relations and marketing are not the same thing; one is not subsumed by the other. But they can work well together.
5. The nature of the changing healthcare environment has made it almost impossible for healthcare organizations to function well without both of these external communication functions.
6. Fund-raising requires well-developed, well-targeted communication campaigns and thus can be considered within the domain of public relations in nonprofit healthcare organizations.
7. If your organization is too small to have a separate public relations function, consider developing a volunteer board consisting of local public relations experts.
8. Public relations in health care is best practiced as an internal activity, but there are some specific occasions when you may require outside PR consultants.

For Your Bookshelf

Coombs, W. Timothy, and Sherry Holladay. *It's Not Just PR: Public Relations in Society*. Malden, MA: Blackwell Publishing, 2007.

Coombs, W. Timothy, and Sherry Holladay. *PR Strategy and Application: Managing Influence*. Malden, MA: Wiley-Blackwell, 2010.

Solis, B., and D. Breakenridge. *Putting the Public Back in Public Relations: How Social Media Is Reinventing the Aging Business of PR*. Upper Saddle River, NJ: Pearson Education, 2009.

On the Web

Canadian Public Relations Society. http://www.cprs.ca
Chartered Institute of Public Relations (UK). http://www.cipr.co.uk/
Institute for Public Relations. http://www.instituteforpr.org/
International Association of Business Communicators. http://www.iabc.com
Public Relations Society of America. http://www.prsa.org

LEVEL III

The World Outside

We are moving toward the top of our strategic pyramid. At the lowest, and broadest, level, we examined your personal communication knowledge, attitudes, and skills as a healthcare manager. We then moved to the internal environment as a first strategic step in creating a healthy communication climate within your organization and solid relationships with a number of important internal groups. Our next level involves extending our sphere of concern and influence to outside the organization.

Healthcare organizations have a wide variety of possible outside audiences and publics. These external stakeholders whose goodwill is important to your organization include potential clients, other healthcare organizations in your community, your geographical neighbourhood, funders, potential funders, and the media. It is possible to consider all of these as your "community."

Level III, then, is devoted to developing lines of communication with your organization's external community, and because of its considerable importance in communicating messages widely, the media.

10 Creating Community Relationships

Always do more than is required of you.

— George S. Patton

How much are your community relationships worth to you? How do you know if those relationships are strong? How important are your own communication skills and public forays in the development of those relationships? If you are unsure about your answers to these questions, then be prepared for a wide variety of problems if you or your organization's relationship with your community is poor.

Poor community relationships can result in some or all of the following:

- poor reputation
- inability to compete
- inability to reach those who require your services
- inability to attract high-quality staff or volunteers
- lack of support for new initiatives
- negative media coverage

And these are just the start.

Unfortunately, many healthcare managers seem to think that the cultivation of community relations is someone else's responsibility. Some consider it to be an issue for their auxiliaries, while others rely completely on their public relations staff to deal with it. The bottom line is that solid community relations begin at the top, not the bottom. As a manager, though, you will want to know that measuring relationships is difficult. Whereas organizations often focus on evaluating their reputation, as demonstrated by the rise in "reputation management specialists," because it is more difficult to accomplish, relationship measurement is not as well developed.[1]

What It Means to Be Part of a Community

Generally, when we refer to our community we are referring to the geographic locality within which we live and work. But *a community is also a collection of people with common interests,* and it is important to think about your community from both perspectives. It is not just that entity that you know as your town, city, or municipality: it is the people who make that geographic entity more than bricks and mortar. They give it life. And your organization is a part of both.

Community relations has been defined in a number of different ways, but it depends on one simple understanding: institutions or organizations are interdependent, functioning as parts of a system. Management's recognition that no organization is an island, and that it needs outside support and sometimes guidance, is fundamental to cultivating good community relationships. Further, interdependence means that each participant expects and needs things from the others. Unfortunately, healthcare organizations often mistakenly believe that they are special cases because their work is somehow on a higher moral ground than, say, a manufacturer. This is a dangerous misconception. Healthcare organizations need to achieve integration into their communities just as do other kinds of institutions. As Professor Warren Burkett pointed out in his now-classic book *News Reporting: Science, Medicine and High Technology,* "All hospitals need to encourage community confidence in them, and to seek to do it through publicity about their successes, equipment, facilities, people, services, and patients."[2]

Another important issue to consider before we get to your own personal role in communication with your community is that of external control. If you are part of an organization that is part of a larger organization without headquarters in your community, then developing a rapport with your community can be an even more crucial challenge. Outside control of an organization, whether real or perceived, can be a source of conflict with the community if this relationship is not cultivated and nurtured.

Your Personal Role

Managers at all levels in healthcare organizations must cultivate an awareness of their outside communities. Your own participation in

.the community and your personal communication skills can have a distinctly positive effect on your organization's relationship with its community.

Public opinion about your organization can be closely related to the communication style that is perceived by the public on many levels. For example, the communication style of the CEO comes directly across to the community in the way he or she responds to the media in crisis, as well as noncrisis, situations. In addition, the style can come across indirectly in the way the community perceives that management treats its employees. Good or bad, these issues can affect public opinion, with all of its implications.

What Your Community Expects from You

Your community expects a variety of things from your organization.

- It expects that you will do what you say you are doing (to "walk the talk" as it were). If you have a publicly proclaimed mission, you need to be perceived to be doing just what that mission says you will do. If the public doesn't know what your mission is, then it is time to ask why, and what you can do to change that.
- It expects that you will provide employment at a fair wage. If you have continuing difficulties with your unions or are accused of unfair labour practices in any way, this will be detrimental to your organization's image. How you communicate about these issues, however, is just as important to the community's perception as the actual issues.
- It expects you to look like a good community citizen. The visual image you portray speaks volumes. Ill-kept buildings or facilities send unintended messages to your community.
- It expects you to act like a good citizen. For example, how do you dispose of your medical refuse? This is an important community issue where actions speak louder than words.
- It expects you to participate in the life of the community. Communities tend to make allowances for healthcare organizations because of the nature of the work done by the professionals and nonprofessionals on site. However, community relations would be enhanced by participation in activities, especially health-related ones. Does your organization have a team in an annual fund-raising run for a particular illness such as breast cancer or HIV? It doesn't have to reflect directly your own mission, but will imply volumes to

the community about your all-around concerns for the health and well-being of the citizens.

- It expects you to communicate in a way it will understand. This is particularly important if any part of your community is actually a sub-public that reflects diversity in cultures – and this applies to almost every kind of health-related organization there is. As one author on the topic of multicultural public relations points out, an organization's relationship with its community should be "inclusive, self-revealing, genuine, personal, and emergent."[3]

These expectations are reasonable and rational. Any organization that values its future will respond to these challenges positively.

Healthcare organizations, just like other organizations, can have different kinds of relationships with their communities. The categorization of the relationship is generally based on the overriding objective: *communal* or *exchange*. Either you want to develop a real sense of community where the relationship is based on mutual trust and shared understandings, or it is a relationship based on the fact that you need something from your community and they need something from you. It is generally believed that relationships that are based on true shared understanding are stronger than those based simply on the need for some kind of exchange.

Corporate Support for Nonprofits

Nonprofit, health-related organizations, whether they provide care, services, education, or research, are often on the other side when it comes to community relations programs. In other words, you may find yourself on the receiving end of a community relations effort that supports the public image of a profit -making corporation (such as a pharmaceutical company). Being a part of a corporation's strategic philanthropy program sounds like a win-win situation. Their image is enhanced, and your organization receives much-needed financial support, equipment, or professional expertise. But does this support your community relations? It depends on several factors.

The first factor to consider is the corporation's profile and reputation – not in its own eyes, but in those of your community. If the organization supporting your efforts has a particularly bad relationship with your community, you might consider doing some research with your own community leaders before partnering with that organization in any way. It could have implications for your own relationship with the community.

Another factor worth considering is whether the corporation's support comes with strings attached – or even when this could be perceived by any of your important stakeholders. It may be a matter of selling only that company's soft drinks on your premises, instead of their competitors', or they may require you to stock only their brand of a particular drug. In any case, can you and your relationships live with their conditions?

If you turn down corporate support for any reason, how will people (including both internal and external groups) perceive your actions? If you are the CEO of a hospital and a tobacco company offers a much-needed financial injection, can you accept it? Is it morally acceptable to take it? To turn it down? Are your communication skills (and those of other managers) up to the task of facing your employees, other donors, your board, your community, and the media?

Indeed, if a nonprofit healthcare organization does become a part of a corporate philanthropy program, managers have roles to play; these roles generally involve communication skills. You may be required to

- appear at news conferences with corporate officials;
- give media interviews;
- speak at corporate functions;
- write articles or be interviewed for their company newsletters, Web sites or blogs; or
- take part in a variety of social functions.

It is not just a simple matter of saying yes!

What You Should Be Doing

Healthcare organizations have always used a wide variety of communication strategies to develop and enhance their relationships with their communities. The public image of health care has, however, changed drastically. As the environment of health services has changed, the public has begun to view many healthcare organizations as part of just another huge, uncaring industry. Communicating with your community to ensure that they do not take this attitude toward your organization is crucial. Healthcare managers can play key roles if their own skills are well honed.

Here are some of the kinds of community relations programs that healthcare organizations develop and implement, and in which healthcare managers can play a significant role.

- *Public information or social marketing campaigns.*[4] Although many of these programs relate to specific health concerns in which health professionals play significant roles as spokespersons, health-care organizations have more recently become concerned about educational campaigns to help consumers navigate the system. Campaigns that focus on healthcare delivery are ideal situations for healthcare managers to get involved. Your involvement can go far beyond the planning of such campaigns – you might consider a role as a spokesperson.
- *Speakers' bureaus.* Many healthcare organizations and facilities have a well-developed speakers' bureau that provides speakers for community groups. Today's consumers and community members are acutely interested in the system as well as in health policy. Healthcare managers at all levels should be a part of this. You can select a topic area in which you are interested and to which you can bring some personal experience. The speakers' bureau administrators (typically the PR department, but it could be anyone) organize the placement. If you don't have one, you might consider developing one. The availability and placement of your speakers can be publicized through your organizational blog, your Twitter account, or more traditional means such as newspaper and radio advertising or public service announcements.
- *Open houses.* Many healthcare organizations occasionally open their doors to their community. This is a terrific opportunity to partici-pate in an effort to help consumers understand the role of man-agement in health care. Many managers place themselves in the background at these times, believing that the community is inter-ested only in front-line health professionals. It doesn't have to be that way. As health care looms larger in the eyes of the community, it needs to see and hear that health care is not a faceless, noncaring industry. Your participation can go a long way to help with this. In addition to these traditional open-door events, online open houses are also useful. At the very least, the traditional open house ought to have an online presence as well.
- *Healthcare facility blog.* Many hospitals, long-term care facilities, and other health-related organization these days maintain blogs. These periodic postings on a variety of topics that are useful to your com-munity can help to nurture long-term relationships. The selection of topics for blogging will be a reflection of the extent to which you value the community's needs over your own communication objectives.

Chapter 10 Key Points

1. Poor relationships with your community can result in a variety of challenges, from a poor reputation (and all that results from that) to an inability to attract and keep good staff.
2. Communication between organizations and their communities is key to that relationship; healthcare managers play a pivotal role.
3. A community can be the traditional geographic kind or the online variety.
4. The general perception of health care is fast becoming one of a faceless, uncaring industry little different from any other service. Community relations can change that.
5. Your community has high expectations of your organization: that you walk the talk, provide employment at a fair wage, and participate within the community. They also expect your organization to both look and act like a good citizen and to communicate with them in a way they understand.
6. If you are part of a nonprofit organization, be careful when the shoe is on the other foot and you are enticed to become part of a corporate strategic philanthropy endeavour.
7. Your own personal communication skills will be key when you are taking your part in community relations programs.

For Your Bookshelf

Bornstein, David. *How to Change the World: Social Entrepreneurs and the Power of New Ideas*. New York: Oxford University Press, 2007.

Makary, Marty. *Unaccountable: What Hospitals Won't Tell You and How Transparency Can Revolutionize Health Care*. New York: Bloomsbury Press, 2012.

On The Web

American Hospital Association. "The Importance of Community Partnerships." CEO Insight Series. http://www.caringforcommunities.org/caringforcommunities/content/10commconn-partnerships.pdf

Kane, Gerald, et al. "Community Relations 2.0." *Harvard Business Review*. http://hbr.org/2009/11/community-relations-20/ar/1

Vancouver Island Health Authority. *Community Relations and Community Review: Report*. http://www.viha.ca/NR/rdonlyres/5962794E-E0CF-4671-BB59-F85F272B6BB0/0/report_comm_review.pdf

11 Media Relations Process and Practices

Four hostile newspapers are more to be feared than a thousand bayonets.
– Napoleon Bonaparte

"Nowhere else are the threads of scientific enterprise more tangled with economic, political, personality, and social values than in medicine and the related health sciences."[1] When Professor Warren Burkett wrote these words in his 1986 book *News Reporting: Science, Medicine and High Technology* to which we have referred previously, he was reflecting on a trend of the 1980s, a trend that has continued into the new century. Medicine and health care are news – in fact, they are big news. As a result, anyone involved in the management of healthcare facilities or services is likely to find that involvement with the media is an inevitable part of getting the job done – a part that cannot be ignored.

Medicine is front-page news. Not a day goes by without some news of a medical drama, health care and the economy, or health care and politics. Medical news does, indeed, have everything that makes for a good news story: human interest, science, personalities, politics, economics, and social values. And with the increasingly blurred lines between information and entertainment – what some commentators refer to these days as "infotainment" – healthcare stories play well, as they say in the media. Although the numbers vary slightly from study to study, and are confounded by coverage of health and medical stories in new media, it is widely accepted that somewhere in the vicinity of 40 per cent of what passes as news is medically related. Add to that number the array of television stories, both fictitious and real, that portray some aspect of health care, and you can safely conclude that many people develop their knowledge and attitudes toward health care largely from mass media – a conclusion that has been supported time and again by research on media consumption habits.

What this means to healthcare managers is that the media are both a conduit through which your organization may need to get its message to a wider public, and also the gatekeepers controlling what does and does not get a wide audience. The relationship that your organization has with the media can have an effect on both your image and the relationships you have with your community, clients and potential clients, government, donors and potential donors, and even your employees and volunteers.

Some healthcare managers, just like most administrative personnel in other industries, believe, mistakenly, that if they simply ignore the media, it will either go away or not affect them. This could not be further from the truth. Regardless of your level within the healthcare hierarchy, there will come a time when either you must face media questions or, at the very least, should use the media to your best advantage. Thus you can take either a reactive or a proactive stance toward your relationship with the media, but I suggest that you consider developing the attitude that the media needs you just as much as you need its goodwill. Furthermore, it can be a very valuable tool for the development of your organization and even of your own career. If you feel confident about your understanding of the media and in your own personal media relations skills, then you are likely to have a considerably decreased fear of dealing with this often powerful ally (or foe).

What "Media Relations" Means in Health Care

There is an old saying that you have probably heard before and that every business person worth his or her salt takes very seriously: *perception is reality.*

What the public (or individuals) believe is true is true for them in all its consequences. Whether or not this perception reflects in any way the actual truth of the situation as you see it, the reaction from the public will be based on their "truth" and not yours. How the public comes to develop their perceptions is often a result of media-generated images. In health care, this is even more likely to be true. A successful healthcare executive has learned that the one who can communicate messages best to large groups of people is more likely to have those messages received as they were intended.

Whether you like it or not, the public is learning about health care from newspapers, magazines, radio, television, Web sites, and social media tools. They are receiving images from hard news stories, human-interest dramas, advertising, and reruns of television programs like *ER* and *House* (and even afternoon soaps like *General Hospital*). Whether or not you as a healthcare manager consider these appropriate sources of information upon which to base opinions doesn't matter – it is the truth. If you and your healthcare organization have cultivated a beneficial relationship with the media, you may find that you have a degree of influence over how the messages are conveyed and interpreted, at least in your immediate geographic area.

Media relations, then, implies the development of long-term relationships between your organization and the media for mutual benefit. This mutuality means that media cooperation can be very important for you, but your cooperation can also be very useful for the media. The two main benefits of good media relations are (1) being able to use the media to get a needed message to the public, and (2) increasing the likelihood of balanced coverage in times of crisis or difficulty.

For example: you are the manager of an emergency department or the administrator of a hospital whose overworked emergency department had to send an incoming ambulance patient to another hospital, and the patient dies. The media will begin covering the story from the perspective of the "poor little guy" – in this case, the patient and his or her family—versus the "big bad guy" – you as a representative of the hospital. A hospital that has cultivated good relationships with the media, and a healthcare manager who is known and trusted by the local media, will have a better chance of a fairer, faster hearing before the story mushrooms out of proportion. But before you can handle an impending crisis like this scenario well, your organization needs to have a well-developed media relations policy.

Media Policies in Health Care

So, the reporters get a tip about the patient who died after being turned away at your emergency department, and they start calling – or worse, arrive on your doorstep. The first person a reporter looks for is a nurse in the emergency department. She starts talking. Then everyone the reporter encounters on his or her way to the official sources talks as well. By the time the reporter reaches you, the story is already juicy-enough to go with – never mind that few of the informers had any first-hand knowledge or even the facts. And the advent of social media has resulted in even more opportunities for the media to collect stories.

Do you let just anyone in your institution talk to the media? Have you even thought about it? Do you let reporters into your long-term care facility to begin filming residents any time they like? Do you try to avoid reporters or give them the official "no comment" response? Do you ever tell a media person something that is really not true to get them off your back? Do you have social media policies governing employee behaviour?

All of these issues must be considered, and organizational policies developed to address them. Media relations policies for the following five very important areas should be developed and fully communicated to all internal groups.

Your Media Liaison

A healthcare organization needs one media liaison as the first point of contact with the media and to designate others as spokespersons on specific issues as the need arises. Both the individual's position within the organizational hierarchy as well as that individual's media presentation skills should be considered in the selection of this person. In a large organization, this official liaison is often a member of the public relations staff whose title reflects his or her position as media relations officer. Anyone working in such a position should have his or her media presentation skills already examined prior to being hired. In smaller organizations, the liaison is often the administrator or another director if that person's skills are more fully developed. Just because you are the head honcho doesn't necessarily mean that you are the best person for the job. The problem here is that reporters often don't want to talk to the media liaison: rather they want to hear from a doctor, nurse, or researcher at the front line of the story. The liaison is then responsible for briefing that other person, who is then designated to speak about a particular subject, and only that subject. As a healthcare manager, however, you should be cultivating and nurturing your own media skills so that you are never in a position where you feel intimidated by the media when you are the spokesperson.

Cooperation and Honesty

The second area of concern in the development of media relations policy is taking the view that your organization and its representatives will always be cooperative and honest with the media. The issue of honesty cannot be stressed enough. Any organization that has ever lied to the media has found itself with a very difficult task of rebuilding any trust that might have existed previously. Being cooperative means returning calls when you say you will and providing as much information as is reasonable and ethical, given the situation.

Confidentiality

The third area of policy derives directly from the issue of openness and honesty, and is of particular concern in healthcare organizations: confidentiality of patient information. Although you need to have a clear confidentiality policy that is lucidly and calmly related to reporters and media outlets, this cannot be the rule that you continually hide behind in an effort to avoid giving out information to the media. Your policy needs to be very clear about what can and cannot be divulged as a matter of organizational policy.

Internal Communication

The next aspect of policy is ensuring that internal audiences receive any information that is being communicated to external audiences *before* that external communication takes place. No employee or volunteer should ever find out about internal activities via mass media – whether traditional (e.g., newspaper or television) or social media (e.g., blogs, online news sources, videos, Twitter). As a matter of policy, you need to find a way to put the internal groups first, and new media can be your ally in this effort. Obviously, in times of crisis, this communication may have to be simultaneous, but the policies and procedures for considering those closest to home first need to be in place.

Internal Policy

Finally, you need to have a way to communicate these policies to all internal publics. It isn't enough to have a policy that says any employee contacted by the media about any organizational matter must first contact the media liaison if the employees don't know that such a policy exists. One of the best ways to communicate these kinds of policies is to develop a media training workshop that provides background information on the media and how to handle situations as they arise. Not everyone needs actual training on how to give a media interview, but everyone could benefit from a better understanding. (See the end of this chapter for a basic outline of what should be covered in a media training workshop.)

Healthcare managers constantly deal with policies of all kinds. Why shouldn't a good media policy be one of them? Most often, such an omission can be attributed to a lack of understanding of what the media really do and how they do it.

Understanding the Media

Isn't it helpful to know something about what that person on the other end of the phone does? Enhancing your understanding of a reporter's job and the environment within which he or she works helps you to improve your ability to get the right message out at the right time – and can greatly enhance your comfort level. Let's begin by looking in general terms at the reporter's media environment and then more specifically at whom that person is and how that person's work is accomplished.

The Media Environment

In very general terms, it is important to understand that today's media are largely event-oriented rather than issue-oriented when it comes to health-related content. By definition, issues are broader, deeper, and have more long-term influence over our lives. There are many important health-related issues, from healthcare delivery methods to funding and medical research priorities. The media, however, are far more likely to hone in on a specific event as it relates to the issue, even if that specific event is not representative of the broader concerns. This one piece of information can help you to understand why reporters sometimes ask you questions that you think are relatively unimportant. Our understanding of this aspect of the media has been bolstered by research.

Some years ago (and it is safe to say that little has changed), a media researcher in Britain analysed the content of 1,397 health-related articles in seven national newspapers. The results pointed directly to the media's orientation toward events rather than issues. The researcher found that 58 per cent of the articles were about an event and gave light details of the surrounding issue. A further 16 per cent of the articles focused on the event as well, but provided enough information about the related issue to give readers some background. Only 26 per cent had a discussion of the issue as their main focus.[2] We might conclude that even if the event is reported objectively, the reader, viewer, or listener is likely to receive a skewed image of the real situation. It is especially true in health and healthcare reporting that one event is never representative of the entire surrounding issue.

So, how are these decisions made? Why does one story get printed or aired, while another is buried? Why is one story front-page news and another left out entirely?

Every basic news writing textbook used by student journalists has its own list of news values: the criteria used to determine the newsworthiness of a particular story. Generally, these values include the following:

- *Timeliness.* "News" is related to "new." If it happened last week, it is not likely to be news unless the remainder of its news values overcomes this. Indeed, this search for timeliness explains why reporters are on your doorstep before you even know there is a story, and why they always have deadlines to drive them.
- *Currency.* This is related to timeliness, but allows for more leeway in when an event actually happened. If the situation is related to an ongoing, current consumer and/or media interest in a particular topic, it has a high level of newsworthiness.
- *Prominence.* The more prominent the individuals involved, the more likely that something is newsworthy. If your next-door neighbour has quadruple by-pass surgery it is not news – unless he happens to be the mayor (or a congressman, or a movie star, etc.).
- *Proximity.* The closer to home an event occurs, the more newsworthy it is. A small story nationally may be a huge story locally. This is also related to prominence. If the chief executive officer of a small, Midwest hospital is accused of sexual harassment, the story likely has little news value for national outlets, but it may be front-page news in the local media.
- *Consequences.* If the situation will have significant consequences, it is more newsworthy. If something small that happens in a long-term care facility is likely to have some public policy outcome, it is now newsworthy.
- *Human drama.* We used to refer to this news value as human interest. More and more, however, there also has to be a dramatic component to the story. Health care is rife with human-interest stories, as well as human dramas.

- *Controversy*. Many journalism textbooks fail to identify this as a real draw for reporters, but anyone who has ever been on the other side of the microphone knows that controversy is compelling to reporters. Indeed, many of us have had the experience of a reporter seeking out a controversy where no apparent one existed.

Knowing about these news values is important to you in two ways. First, it helps you to understand why some stories that you think are important never make it to the front page. Second, it helps you to understand the direction of the questioning that you will inevitably face when a reporter comes calling. In the end, decisions about what plays in the media on any given day are affected by the gatekeeping role of the media outlets and their employees

Journalists Are People, Too

Once you understand a bit about the environment that guides the work of the media that you see every day, dealing with the media as a healthcare manager requires you to understand something about that person who is asking all the questions.

The face of journalism has changed considerably. Fifty years ago, you would probably have faced a man who had learned his trade by coming up through the ranks. He was probably a bit left-wing in his political leanings, and if we are to believe the kernel of truth in any public stereotype, perhaps he was just a bit ill-kempt.

Journalists today are well educated. Most have studied journalism, among other things, at college or university. The person holding a microphone in your face today is just as likely to be a woman, and she may be representative of even more diverse backgrounds than you would have faced years ago.

It can sometimes be difficult when, as an executive, you are faced with a person who believes that he or she has a mission as a seeker of the truth. You need to ensure that you are not put off by the possibility that this person might just take the moral high ground, and it may be difficult for you to reclaim even footing. But the reality is that while it would seem that the traditional value of objectivity in reporting would make that moral high ground unnecessary, today's journalistic imperative is closer to taking the side of the so-called little guy against the big guy and seeking the story's balance from that initial stance.

This potentially slanted view is an interesting dichotomy for reporters today as they deal with the conflict between their desire to represent
the truth as they see it, and their need to be loyal to their profit-seeking
bosses. Keep in mind that media outlets (apart from public broadcast-
ing) are not nonprofits.

Another way to understand a journalist's perspective is to determine
if a specific journalist takes an "audience advocate" role (little guy versus big guy as noted above) or a "skeptic's role." Journalists who take
on the role of audience advocate seem to be more open to information
generated by the healthcare organization, rather than feeling that this
information is biased[AQ1].[3]

Finally, however, journalists are people who are just doing their jobs.
As media trainer and former journalist Ed Shiller once said:

> Aside from the stereotype of the reporter as ill-groomed and ill-clothed,
> one of the most persistent perceptions of your local reporter is that he or
> she is either out to get a story, no matter whose toes are trampled, or is an
> unprincipled sensationalist who wants to nail you to the cross ... but most
> reporters are not out to get you. They're out to get a legitimate story.[4]

The Medium Is the Message?

If Marshall McLuhan was right, and the medium is truly the message,
then it behooves anyone who plans to have any dealings with mass
media to understand how each medium differs and how that medium
can alter the message you intended.

Consider this situation. Some years ago, I had a position heading
up the communication program for a large multiorgan transplant service. The nature of organ procurement and the fact that organ trans-
plantation was still a media darling at the time meant that I spent many
hours giving interviews, appearing on television, and answering the
public's questions on radio call-in shows, among other things.

I received a call one morning from an enterprising young reporter
from a local affiliate of a national television station. It seemed that the
reporter had been contacted by the leader of a grass-roots community
group that had been lobbying for the implementation of an organ donor
registry. I was very familiar with this group, having met with them several times to determine how we could work together. This collaborative
approach was tempered by my own research on organ donor registries,

focusing on where they had been tried in the past. There were no success stories. However, it was not our habit to squash a community effort to enhance organ donation without a genuine attempt to work together.

The reporter arrived in my office with her cameraman, and before we began my on-camera interview, she told me that she had already interviewed the head of the citizen's group and would be using portions of each interview. We started with a general discussion of the organ donation process, yet again, and the notion of an organ donor registry. I related to her some of the information I had gleaned from my research on the topic. When she asked about our apparent lack of action on the development of the registry as this group of concerned citizens wished, I assured her that we had been meeting regularly, and although these registries had never worked in the past, we were interested in cooperating in any way we could with citizens who supported our work. There was no fight here.

I sat in front of my television at six o'clock that evening to see the results of this interview. My twenty-minute interview resulted in two twenty-second clips that had been craftily edited and juxtaposed with remarks made by the leader of the citizens' group so that the story seemed to be one of conflict between the "big hospital complex" that was being noncooperative and the "good guy" citizens who just wanted to help. Had the interview been live on the radio, the message would have been quite different. Clearly, understanding the differences between the various types of media can help you to hone your media relations skills and anticipate possible misrepresentation.

The Printed Word

Print media, the granddaddy of all the mass media we are familiar with today, is still an important part of how a large proportion of your publics will receive information about you and your organization. These days you can also expect that the story will have a life in cyberspace since most newspapers have an online version. Once the story is posted online, it can take on a life of its own: a life that is forever. Therefore, for better or for worse, the potential reach of your message is even greater than it used to be.

In general terms, the newspaper is looking for what they call "hard news." They want just the facts because the news story has a short life span (here today, gone tomorrow). This is still generally true, although many newspapers are increasingly including longer, more in-depth pieces to feed the information needs of their readers, and to compete with other sources of information such as magazines and television.

Magazines, although increasingly electronic in nature, but still an important print medium, have a longer story life, their stories involve more research on the part of the writers and researchers, and they can present an analysis. A reporter interviewing you for a news story may ask you about some of the background so that he or she can understand, but much of that background will never make it into the story. Magazines as well as feature articles (as opposed to hard news) in newspapers can take a more creative approach as they fill up considerably more space.

An interview for print media can be either via the telephone or in person, or even via a Skype™ call these days. Although the telephone interview generally takes up less of your time, you are at a disadvantage (as is your interviewer) since you can't see their body language and facial expressions. Either way, you can make your points (we will get to that).

Lights, Camera ...

Television (and online video) is almost endlessly varied these days. News broadcasts tend to use short stories, much like a newspaper in that they want just the facts, but they prefer to have a visual context and the story is subject to aggressive editing, as my case suggested. The visual aspect of television news stories can sometimes present a challenge to health facilities whose primary responsibility is to protect the privacy of their clients or patients. While a TV crew may wish to walk around and creatively take footage of anything they like, this is impossible. Therefore, your policies must not only cover this possibility, but must also be conveyed to the appropriate media personnel.

Aside from news stories on television, there is a vast array of other types of pieces and shows in which you might become involved. Feature broadcasts, such as news magazine shows, can use either short or long stories, but they always include both visuals as well as talk. The continual, uninterrupted "talking head" is really past its day as audiences have become more sophisticated and visually demanding. These kinds of broadcasts are carefully scripted, and the editing is creative, to say the least. An interviewee generally has no idea how this will come out on the other end.

Some kinds of television interviews that you might be asked to do include

- *The talk show*. These range from your local noon-hour, in-studio discussion with a broadcaster to the confrontational style of talk show that has become popular in recent years. Generally, however, these interviews involve actually sitting down in a studio with an interviewer. As you are being interviewed in this situation, you need to ensure that you talk to the interviewer, not to the camera.
- *The headshot*. The camera will look directly at you while you talk into it apparently to a host whom the audience cannot see. The interviewer's questions are usually edited out. This could be taped in your office, on the street outside your hospital, in the hallway, or, less likely, in the studio.
- *The news magazine*. This will be a more in-depth interview. The crew might even follow you around for a while. They will want to see you in action. Then they will go away and shoot others and edit them together into a television magazine story.
- *The scrum*. This happens when you are confronted with a number of reporters, usually just as you walk out a door from a meeting of one sort or another. It happens to politicians all the time, but it can also happen to you. If you are negotiating with a union for their new contract, if you have made an on-camera presentation to a government inquiry, or if something controversial is happening inside your institution, you will inevitably run into reporters waiting for a comment.
- *The ambush*. This comes from an individual reporter (although it could be more) who waits somewhere (like around a corner as you are walking to your car) to surprise you, usually shoving a microphone or digital recorder in your face to get a comment from you.
- *The double-ender*. This happens when you are actually being interviewed by a broadcaster whose voice you hear through an earpiece and whom you cannot see. To the viewers, it seems that the interviewer is looking directly at you through the magic of a screen beside him or her and that you are looking directly at the interviewer. In fact, you are looking directly into a camera lens. Shift

your eyes away for a split second, and the audience will think you are not to be trusted. The greatest difficulty posed here is the need to focus intently on the interviewer's question. In TV outlets using older equipment, there can even be a delay between the time that the audience hears the question and when you hear it, causing you to look just a bit stunned as you listen intently to what the audience perceives as dead air.

Radio ... After All These Years

Media opportunities for radio come in almost as many varieties as do those for television. There are similarities in some of the interviews, like scrums and ambushes, except that the audience can't see you. News broadcasts on the radio are very short. Each story runs thirty to sixty seconds, and they have an extremely short lifespan. It is a fast-paced, information-oriented environment.

Documentary-type radio shows come and go in popularity. Just now there seems to be resurgence in audience interest, frequently on public broadcasters. Radio documentaries vary considerably in length and depth of coverage. They do, however, rely heavily on ambient sound. If they want to do a story about an intensive care unit, for example, they will want to record sounds of ventilators swishing, heart monitors beeping, even the loudspeaker if you still have one. These documentaries are carefully scripted, and you could be interviewed not only by a broadcaster but also by a background, off-air researcher.

There are essentially four types of radio interviews:

1. *The studio interview*. This is usually for a radio talk show. It will entail a discussion between you and your interviewer. While it might be aired in its entirety, parts of the interview could be taken out for additions to related news stories.
2. *The sound bite*. This is the brief clip of a memorable few words craftily put together that says it all for the interviewer. It is taken from a larger interview, which could be long or short, on the phone or in the studio, or on the street into a digital recorder.
3. *Phone-in shows*. These are obviously live broadcasts, where you are the invited expert in a particular topic area, and listeners are asked to call you with their comments and questions. This is especially fertile ground for health-related topics. You need to be careful what you say, especially if you are being asked for health-related advice.

You also need to know if the station has a broadcast delay: can they bleep out a person's comments before they get onto the air? You can do this in a station with a host, or you can do it in your living room on the telephone for an hour, which will sound just like you are sitting beside the host. (I have done call-in shows while on the East coast, for a live broadcast on the West coast.)

4. *Telephone interviews.* These are very common types of radio interviews, and they can be either live or taped. Live ones are obviously used in their entirety, and you need to be immediately available when the producer calls to get you on the line. Taped phone interviews usually allow you to have a brief chat with the interviewer just before you begin. Sometimes you can even start over if there are any problems at the outset.

So, now that you know something about the backstage aspects of the medium that you will be facing, you are ready to answer that call from a reporter. Or are you?

Help! A Reporter Is Calling

Even if you have little interest in being interviewed by a member of the media, the day will come when you can no longer avoid it. When the reporter calls …

- Stay calm.
- Write down the caller's full name, position, and affiliation.
- Find out the specific purpose of the call.
- Find out what he or she already knows about the issue at hand.
- Ask about the story's deadline.
- If you don't have all the information you need, arrange a call-back.
- Write out your central message and two or three important points.
- Ensure that you have the right to be talking to the media about the topic. Contact your public relations department or your media liaison if you have one.

You're On!

How are your skills in dealing with the media? Even the most seasoned public speaker who can absorb audiences in person, or a personable manager who has terrific rapport with his or her employees, often has difficulty in translating those skills to the specialized area of media presentation. Let's examine general aspects of both your verbal and non-verbal presentation and then look at the specifics of what to do when the media call.

Verbal

The goal of your verbal presentation is to state your message as clearly as possible so that the audience understands and remembers your message. Here are some guidelines that might help.

- *First, know your subject.* Never agree to a media interview on a subject that you know little about. Ensure that you are, indeed, the person to whom the media should be speaking on this subject. Unless you are the CEO, you will need to determine that you have permission from your organization to represent it in the media.
- *Use plain language,* and *speak in relatively short sentences,* each of which should contain only one point. You may think that this is important only when speaking on television or on radio, but it is equally important when giving an interview to a print journalist. Keep in mind that the writer of the story has far less background in this subject than you do and will need to be brought up to speed. *Avoid industry jargon* and medical or technical terms. If you need to use one, explain it briefly before going on.
- Overall, *make only one to three points,* which should have been prepared before the interview. Do not try to make things up as you go along. If you make numerous points, you are essentially leaving it up to the reporter to decide on the priorities and his or her decision may not resemble yours at all. You run the risk of diluting your message.
- *Don't spoil the reporter's "quotable quote" or "sound bite"* by either numbering your points or using the reporter's name (in fact, try to avoid using the reporter's name at all). This is obviously more important in broadcast than in print interviews, but it is easier to be consistent.
- *Never lose control of the tone of your voice.* You may be saying more than you intend, and the reporter will interpret your comments on the basis of both what you say and how you say it.

- *Never actually say "no comment."* It is useless to everyone and when reported verbatim implies to the readers, viewers, or listeners that you are trying to hide something. Instead, indicate that you are unable to give an answer at this time because of ... and give a reason.
- *Never say anything to a reporter "off the record."* There is no such thing. Even though a credible reporter will not actually use your comments, the fact that he or she knows something will slant questions he or she may ask you or others. In fact, one of the most interesting reporters' tactics is to seek corroboration from someone else for a fact that cannot be attributed to the original source because it was "off the record." Thus, your comment can end up in the story anyway, even though it may not be attributed to you.
- *Don't ever guess.* Never, never, never. If you don't know the answer, offer to find someone who does. Guessing can lead to misinformation and place you and your organization in a negative position.
- *Be as honest as is possible* without compromising your organization's need to protect the privacy of patients, clients, staff, board members, physicians, or anyone else to whom you owe this obligation. Simply stated, never, ever lie to the media.

Nonverbal

Whereas all of these suggestions will improve your verbal presentation in an interview situation, your nonverbal presentation has its own issues. Your goal here is to ensure that how the interviewer and/or the audience sees you is congruent with the message that you are trying to convey, as well as the image that you need to project as a representative of your organization. While nonverbal presentation is critical in television interviews because the audience can see you, don't forget your nonverbal communication even when only the interviewer can see you. Here are some mostly visual-medium-related suggestions for your nonverbal presentation.

First, avoid extremes of dress. This includes colour, pattern, and style. Avoid white as it is too reflective for the camera, red because it shimmers on camera, and stripes because they look hallucinogenic to the viewers. Men who are being interviewed late in the day should shave before appearing on camera. That so-called five-o'clock shadow can make you look sinister. Women should avoid short skirts, and both men and women need to remember to pull the back of their jackets down (even sit on the end of it if you can) to avoid that quarterback look. Wear only conservative jewellery, and avoid anything that will clink.

Be constantly aware of your body language and facial expressions. How you physically present yourself can speak more loudly than any words that come out of your mouth. Even gestures or expressions you are not aware of can say volumes about you, so be aware of them at all times.

Avoid waving your hands around or moving them much at all. It is very distracting for the audience. If you tend to "talk with your hands," practise being interviewed, and have someone videotape you. You may never have this problem again after you have seen yourself.

Even if you are not a hand talker, it is a terrific idea to have someone video record you anyway. You might be surprised by what you didn't know about yourself. Do you ever begin your answers with any of these phrases: "I'm glad you asked me that ...," "Well, let me see ...," or any other cliché comments? Are you ever impatient at seemingly dumb questions? Do you ever lose your cool? Do you ever lose eye contact with the interviewer? Are your gestures too noticeable? Do you fiddle? Do you say "uh" a lot? You can learn a lot from the exercise.

Dealing with a Confrontational Reporter

The truth is that most of the time it is actually fun to be interviewed. Sometimes, however, especially when you are dealing with a controversial situation, it isn't enjoyable at all, and, like Mother Theresa, you may feel that "It is harder to face the media than to bathe a leper."

As you develop a good rapport with your local journalists, and they come to see you as a cooperative and effective interviewee, you will run less risk of facing a truly confrontational reporter. Some reporters, however, have this style about them even on the best days. In addition, a reporter may have a hidden agenda and attempt to get you to say something or corroborate something that isn't immediately apparent. Dealing with these reporters can be a challenge.

First, remain calm. You are the expert, and the reporter needs your comments to be able to develop the story. Even if the reporter tries to put you on the defensive, it does you no good to take the bait. Never lose your cool. You can always turn a negative question into a positive answer. When the focus is on a crisis in your organization, for example, focus your answer on the positive steps being taken to deal with the situation.

If the interview is on the telephone, it is even easier to deal with a confrontational reporter. Be very polite and indicate to the reporter that you are out of time but that you would be happy to continue the interview later. This will give you time to prepare.

Many managers in healthcare organizations seem to think that all reporters are likely to be confrontational. This isn't true at all – but from time to time you will face one who is, and you need to be prepared.

Do You Need Media Training?

Most healthcare managers should be specifically trained in media presentation at some point in their careers. Certainly, it is necessary for high-level executives in health-related organizations to have more than a passing understanding of the media and how they appear in the media. But is media training cost effective?

In most cases, the answer to that question is yes. However, the training you need may be available to you from your own public relations staff. If you are part of an organization that is large enough to have such a staff, they should be able to do this. If you are flush with money, you might even consider hiring a specialist from outside your organization who can do this for you and a group of managers. It just might help you avoid public embarrassment in the future.

If you have less money, you might consider tracking down a faculty member from your local college or university public relations department or corporate communication program. These people often have a great deal of experience and are far less expensive than media training firms. They might not provide as slick a presentation, but it will be just as effective.

What should you expect from a media trainer? You might hire a media trainer for one-on-one counselling, but for a group situation you should have a presentation about the media and how to present yourself, as well as a role-playing experience. Each participant in such a workshop should have an opportunity to be interviewed, videotaped, and critiqued. This is the part that can make media training expensive.

Figure 11.1 suggests a typical outline for a brief but comprehensive media training session. It is also a reasonable summary of what you need to know to be personally ready to deal with the media.

Figure 11.1 Sample Media Training Workshop Guideline

Defining "Good Media Relations"

- benefits of good media relations
- Components of solid media relations policy
- a managerial responsibility

Health and Health Care in Media

- Why health stories "play well"

Understanding Media

- profile of the journalist
- journalistic interview techniques
- types of interviews: print, TV, radio
- How each medium differs
- What makes news
- the citizen journalist (blogs)

The Interview

- why you should do during the interview
- How to prepare for an interview
- Verbal presentation
- nonverbal presentation
- what not to do during an interview

Dealing with the Confrontational Journalist

On-Camera Role Play

- each participant is interviewed and taped
- each interview is played to the group for evaluation

Chapter 11 Key Points

1. Health and health care are newsworthy, and healthcare managers cannot afford to ignore the media.
2. All healthcare managers should be trained in media presentation as they climb the organizational hierarchy.
3. Healthcare organizations need well-articulated media relations policies that are communicated clearly both internally and to the media.
4. Most health-related stories in the media are event oriented rather than issue oriented, which does not always lend itself to the audience's full understanding of the context.
5. Journalists today are well educated and more diverse in gender, ethnic background, and political leanings.
6. It is important to understand the different types of interviews for various media.
7. Always prepare carefully for a media interview.
8. If media interviews are or should be a part of your job today or in the future, get thee to a media trainer!

For Your Bookshelf

Howard, Carol, and Wilma Matthews. *On Deadline: Managing Media Relations.* Long Grove, IL: Waveland Press, 2006.
Seale, Clive, ed. *Health and the Media.* Malden, MA: Wiley-Blackwell Publishing, 2004.

On the Web

American Medical Writers' Association. http://www.amwa.org/default.asp?Mode=DirectoryDisplay&id=1&DirectoryUseAbsoluteOnSearch=True
Association of Healthcare Journalists. http://www.healthjournalism.org/
Foremski, Tom. *Why Social Media Releases Are Moving in a Bad Direction – Questionable Ethics in Masquerading as "News"* http://www.siliconvalleywatcher.com/mt/archives/2007/10/why_social_medi.php
"Preparing for the Media Interview." http://www.fullcirc.com/rlc/media interviewprep.htm
Thomas, P. *Thirteen Tips for Great Media Interviews.* http://www.pantaneto.co.uk/issue28/thomas.htm

LEVEL IV

Crises and Issues

Tracking and managing issues, preparing for, dealing with, and preventing crises: these are all in a day's work for managers in any industry today, including health care. Frequently, however, many managers fail to recognize the strategic value of full consideration of communication in such situations and how their own communication skills and style could affect the outcomes – for better or for worse.

In this final level, we will examine communication in crisis and issue situations, and take a look at the future of strategic communication for healthcare managers.

12 Communication in a Crisis

From fortune to misfortune is a short step; from misfortune to fortune is a long way.

– Yiddish proverb

When a crisis hits a health-related organization, the managers are front and centre. Quite apart from how you manage the operational aspects of the crisis, communication during these times of stress can make or break the success of the operations and have long-term consequences. Communicating during a crisis is not the same as everyday communication. Although it is important to consider all of the same audiences, what you need to say and how you need to say it are two different things. Will you be ready when it hits the fan?

What Is a Crisis, Anyway?

Like much modern jargon, the term *crisis* is often used when a less extreme word will do, when the situation is not really a crisis at all. So what actually constitutes a crisis?

As you read crisis management literature, you will come to one striking conclusion: everyone who writes about it seems to have a different interpretation of the word. While some experts in communications equate a crisis with catastrophes, disasters, and other events that could only be described as dire, others take a broader view. Webster's is, however, very clear in its definition about the important characteristic of a crisis: "... a turning point in the progress of an affair or of a series of events; a critical moment."[1] It is this quality of the potential for important consequences that turns a situation into a crisis – and frequently that situation is indeed derived from a series of events that are already happening.

American communication scholar Professor Timothy Coombs wraps up the diverse definitions this way:

> A crisis is the perception of an unpredictable event that threatens important expectancies of stakeholders and can seriously impact an organization's performance and generate negative outcomes.[2]

His addition of the issue of the public's *perception* of the event is what makes good communication in a crisis essential – it is these communicated ideas and images that contribute to the perceptions.

Public relations professional Albert Tortorella has consulted with a wide variety of organizations facing crises, including Johnson and Johnson during the Tylenol crisis and Union Carbide when it faced its Bhopal tragedy. He put it this way: "A problem which may be on the agenda for future action becomes a crisis when it is pushed into the present ahead of its schedule. Often the pushing ... comes from the media."[3] It is this vulnerability of public exposure with its potential consequences that forces that issue into the forefront. So, for the purposes of our discussion about healthcare communication during a crisis, we will define a crisis as follows:

> A crisis is an event of considerable urgency that opens a health-related organization to public scrutiny outside its control and which has potentially serious consequences for the organization's image and its ability to fulfil its mission.

In health-related organizations, the potential crises are many, from those that are specific to the healthcare industry, to those that can befall any organization. Here are some examples of crises that have occurred in healthcare organizations:

- strikes
- layoffs
- an on-premises shooting
- discovery of a dead doctor in the OR lounge (suicide)
- arrest of a nurse for allegedly killing babies in the NICU
- a lost patient

- a medication error resulting in the death of a patient
- a lawsuit or potential lawsuit
- a bomb threat
- an activist attack on an animal research facility
- alleged misappropriation of funds by a senior manager
- allegations of patient/resident bashing
- serious ethical questions about a new technology
- an outbreak of a serious contagion

Although clearly some of these situations can happen in any kind of an organization, others are specific to health and medicine. The managers who would be involved in these crises include the front-line managers directly involved, as well as their supervisors and, often indirectly, managers on their same level in other departments. As you have probably already figured out, media attention can add considerably to the gravity of the situation from your point of view. Thus, information and how it is communicated are key issues when dealing with a crisis. How you and your organization come across to the public can have more far-reaching consequences than how your organization handles the situation from an operational perspective. Remember: *perception is reality*.

Maintaining Credibility

Crises tend to generate a lot of contradictory information from a wide variety of sources, many of which you have no control over. What you can control, however, is the quality of the information coming from your organization and how it is conveyed. How you are perceived by the public during a crisis is its reality; therefore, it is critical for you to appear credible and honest. Although being honest and appearing credible are related, they aren't the same thing.

If you and your organization have paid careful attention to your relationships with your community and the media, and you have a reputation for honesty and fairness, you are ahead of the game during a crisis. A solid reputation is one of the most important assets you can take into the public eye in the middle of a crisis. After that, your organization's and your own personal ability to communicate honestly and fairly with the media and other publics during the critical period of time will either enhance or detract from your credibility.

Communicating During a Crisis

It is widely believed in communications circles that if you don't "go public" within the first three to six hours after a crisis becomes public you have very little chance of recovering your credibility or of taking control of a situation. That old-school belief was seriously undermined in the wake of the Virginia Tech massacre in 2007 when students and the public took to social media tools like YouTube to disseminate information even as the crisis communication plan was beginning to play out. That changed crisis communication planning forever.

Therefore, being prepared for the worst is important. This means that both you and your organization need to think about crises long before they happen.

Communication during a crisis requires three main elements: *two plans (one for managing the crisis and one for communication), a competent crisis communication team,* and *a credible spokesperson.*

Having a crisis plan at your fingertips requires continual scanning of your organization's environment to determine possible issues that could escalate into crises. For example, if your hospital has a research facility that uses animals in their work, you would need to be prepared for any escalation of animal-rights activity. This means that your public relations personnel need to be proactive, forging appropriate community relationships and preparing a plan to use should the need arise. This is a specific issue that can escalate. But what if an estranged spouse walks into your staff lounge and shoots his wife? You could not have been expected to be prepared for this specific event that is not unique to health care. That is why communication must be an important element in the development of your generic crisis management plan.

Here is what should happen to your organization's communication when a crisis hits:

- Immediately appoint an official spokesperson.
- Assemble all the factual and background material available.
- Assemble your crisis communication team.
- Prepare your key messages (no more than three).
- Communicate important information to your employees and other important internal publics (this may involve a plan to use internal social media).
- Respond to the media quickly and efficiently.
- Consider all other affected stakeholders, and communicate with them quickly (more about this later).

- Never, ever lie to any of your stakeholders.
- Avoid prattling on about the issues at hand.
- Avoid becoming defensive.
- Be proactive, and keep control of the communication as much as possible.
- Keep your communication simple and free of health, medical, or hospital jargon.
- Avoid saying "no comment," and, as usual when dealing with the media, never say anything "off the record."
- Continually monitor how the crisis is being reported in the media, both traditional and online.

The bottom line is that if you have established a good reputation, enhanced your organization's and your own communication skills, and prepared for the worst, communicating during a crisis is a matter of maintaining your composure and using the skills that you would use on a regular basis. These skills need to be applied not only to media interactions, but to communication with any of your stakeholders whose responses could have an effect on your future relationship with them.

Dealing with Your Stakeholders

If you are in the habit of considering the effect of your actions and words on all those groups whose goodwill is important to your organization, then considering their needs during a crisis will come naturally. However, if you are concerned only with what the media might say, then you will almost certainly cause a deterioration in your relationship with any number of other important publics.

First, consider your employees. As we have discussed previously, they are your most important ambassadors and should be considered as such during a crisis. Ensure that employees are kept informed. If you are a front-line manager, take it upon yourself to become the liaison who accumulates the factual information to quell the rumours that inevitably develop during a crisis. If you are a higher-level manager, then ensure that your front-line managers have the information they need.

If you have a board of directors, careful consideration must be made to keep them in the communication loop. It is possible that the chairman of your board may consider him or herself to be an unofficial spokesperson for your organization. This is a mistake. Board chairs, or board members for that matter, are not involved in the day-to-day activities of your organization and need to be made aware before the fact that their role during a crisis is minimal. If you do have a staff member such as a physician on your board, you need to be very forthright about that person's role in public communication during a crisis.

You will also need to pay attention to other groups during a crisis, assessing their communication needs and strategically responding to their informational requirements. The most important of these groups include your patients or clients and their families, and the community in which you function. These will always be important groups. Then, depending upon the type of crisis, you may also need to consider government or regulatory agencies, activist groups, unions, or any other specifically involved group. Communication with these groups cannot be left to the media. In other words, these groups should receive their information in a less-filtered way from your organization.

Methods used to communicate with these groups vary with the group and your objectives, but perhaps even more important is that the practicalities of a crisis situation may require you to alter your ideal. For example, although it may be strategically optimum for you to speak directly to your internal groups on a daily basis as a lengthy crisis unfolds, this may not be feasible. Thus, you may need to utilize electronic communication methods such as e-mail.

Being the Spokesperson: Are You Ready?

Unless you are in the position of chief administrator or director of communication, it is unlikely that you will be the official spokesperson. However, as a healthcare manager, you may be called upon by that official spokesperson to speak for your organization if the crisis directly affects your managerial unit or you are, in fact, the on-site expert about a specific, related issue. In either event, you need to have a handle on your own skills as a spokesperson.

In your role as a spokesperson, the group you will have the most interaction with is the media. As you do a self-assessment, then, you should go back to the basic media skills that we examined in our discussion of media relations. However, during a crisis, while general techniques may be the same, challenges can be heightened.

During a crisis, perhaps more than during any other kind of situation, it is important to ensure that the media "get it right." This means that monitoring the media is extremely important. Further, it is important to follow up if, indeed, there are errors in the reporting. How do you do this?

First, check your facts, then go directly to the reporter who made the mistake. This is not the time to be lodging a complaint with the *Broadcast Standards Council* or *Press Council*. That approach will only serve to anger the reporter and further erode your increasingly frail relationship with him or her. Once you are certain that your complaint has foundation, contact that reporter and calmly and diplomatically describe the nature of your concern: an unbalanced story, a factual error, a misleading slant. Between the two of you, you may be able to determine a mutually agreeable solution.

If the reporter adamantly refuses to see the error as being something that he or she should address, you will then have to consider alternative approaches. This usually involves a pointed letter to the editor (back to your writing skills); or in a very difficult situation, you may have to consider a paid advertisement (print or broadcast) from your organization. In addition, you will consider using your organization's official social media channels such as your Facebook page or your Twitter account to correct mistakes. Paid advertising, it needs to be said, has both advantages and disadvantages. The main advantage in an advertisement is that you have complete control over the message, both verbally and visually, and the size of the story that will appear. The disadvantage is that the public often views such advertising sceptically. Without the perception of third-party endorsement, the message loses a degree of credibility. Obviously, the more credible you and your organization are in the eyes of your community in general, the more likely that any message from you will be perceived as more honest.

What is interesting about strategic communication during a crisis is that a manager's skills in interpersonal and written communication, and the ability to deal with the media, can have long-term effects on the outcomes.

Lessons Learned

There is much to be learned from those who have successfully navigated the stormy waters of crises in healthcare institutions.

In 2003, Toronto was hit with an unexpected outbreak of SARS.[4] The Sunnybrook and Women's College Health Science Centre was in the thick of the crisis. Craig DuHamel, vice president of public affairs, articulated a series of lessons that are useful for any healthcare manager facing a crisis situation.

> ... start by building strong relationships ... banking as much credibility as possible ... look for milestones along the way and keep the internal public motivated and informed ... never wait to communicate all of the facts ... realize early on that the PR department is not the only area in an organization responsible for communication. Mid- to senior-level leaders must assume a communicator's role and help fan out messages internally and externally.[5]

The lessons learned in other industries in other times of crisis are just as important in health care.

The year 2007 ushered in the era of socially mediated crisis communication, offering managers both opportunities and problems. On 16 April 2007, a shooter began a rampage on the campus of Virginia Polytechnic Institute and State University (Virginia Tech) in Blacksburg, Virginia. When the rampage ended, thirty-two students were dead, and the shooter had committed suicide. The international media attention and subsequent public discussions about American gun laws and the treatment of the mentally ill were arguably not the real legacy; the real legacy was the change it brought about in crisis communication.

Within minutes of the shooting, students began updating their new Facebook pages and uploading cell-phone videos to YouTube. The university did not inform students about the first of two shooting sessions. By then, the university had lost all semblance of control of the messages. It was a lesson that has prompted changes across sectors in how communication is dealt with in the aftermath of a crisis. Because in the end, the aftermath is what is important after the crisis has passed.

Chapter 12 Key Points

1. Communication during a crisis is an important strategic consideration.
2. Managers in healthcare organizations require high-level communication skills to have a positive effect on the outcome of a crisis.
3. Media involvement is inevitable in crisis situations.
4. Maintaining credibility with all stakeholder groups, including your internal groups, is crucial to an organization successfully weathering a crisis.
5. It is important to "go public" within the first few hours during a crisis to maintain control and credibility.
6. Strategic communication during a crisis requires a plan, a crisis team, and a spokesperson.
7. Don't forget about communication with internal groups when a crisis has made a situation public.
8. The advent of social media has changed the ability of organizations to take control of communication in a crisis.

For Your Bookshelf

Henry, Rene A. *You'd Better Have a Hose if You Want to Put Out the Fire: The Complete Guide to Crisis and Risk Communications.* Windsor, CA: Golly wobbler Productions, 2000.

Johnson, R., and R. Brown. *Crisis Communication: Case Studies in Healthcare Image Restoration.* Marblehead, MA: Healthleaders Media, 2006.

Ulmer, R., T. Sellnow, and M. Seeger. *Effective Crisis Communication: Moving from Crisis to Opportunity.* 2nd ed. Thousand Oaks, CA: Sage Publications, 2011.

On the Web

Coombs, Timothy. *Crisis Management and Communications.* Institute for Public Relations. http://www.instituteforpr.org/topics/crisis-management-and-communications/

Ontario Health Plan for an Influenza Pandemic (August 2008). http://www.health.gov.on.ca/english/providers/program/emu/pan_flu/ohpip2/ch_12a.pdf

Public Safety and Homeland Security Bureau. *Sample Crisis Communication Plans.* http://publicsafety.fcc.gov/pshs/clearinghouse/index.htm?section=Communication%20Plans

Seeger, Matthew. "Best Practices in Crisis Communication: An Expert Panel Process." *Journal of Applied Communication Research* 34, no. 3 (August 2006): 232–44. http://people.oregonstate.edu/~flayb/MY%20COURSES/H549%20Mass%20Media%20and%20Health%20-%20Winter%202012/Weekly/Week%208%20-%20Seeger.Best%20Practices.pdf

13 A View to the Future

When they discover the center of the universe, a lot of people will be disappointed to discover they are not in it.

– Bernard Bailey

No organization functions in a vacuum. Neither does the world revolve around any single organization. No matter how noble the cause, how admirable the work, how worthy the protagonists, there will always be detractors, critics, and sceptics. Health-related organizations, perhaps more than any others, and particularly some health professionals, often suffer from the mistaken idea that because of the human service aspect of the work they do, they somehow have a right to the higher moral ground. This is a dangerous assumption for healthcare managers. What is needed more than ever before is careful consideration of how health-related organizations and their managers appear to the public.

The need for strategic communication in the management of healthcare activities has grown out of a need for organizations to communicate their messages expertly to a variety of constituents whose goodwill is important. This goes far beyond trying to persuade publics to your point of view, as we have discussed throughout this book. The behaviour of these constituents both directly and indirectly affects the organization's ability to continue pursuing its noble cause, its admirable work, and its overall service to society. And the need for this approach to strategic communication will only intensify, rather than diminish, in the future.

To examine the future of communication within healthcare management we need to broaden our view. Examining the role of health-related organizations within a social context provides us with an expansive canvas upon which to paint a vision of the future. Change is inevitable; therefore, a serviceable starting point is a look at what is likely to be transformed on this canvas. However, some issues are not likely to change a great deal, and these are just as important. Finally, we will look at how the individual healthcare manager can keep his or her communication strategic.

Things That Will Change

There are some things that will change and some things that will remain the same. Let's begin by examining some of the things that will undoubtedly change.

The Aging Population

Probably one of the most important factors affecting how healthcare organizations must reconsider how they communicate is the aging population. No one needs the government statistics about the aging baby boomers to recognize that the population is getting older. This situation is particularly acute for healthcare organizations, since health problems increase with age. The communication strategies and approaches of both organizations and individuals will have to change.

First, the age of your employees is edging ever upward: Workers aged fifty-five and older are the fastest growing segment of the workforce, with the median age of the Canadian workforce having finally reached over forty in 2006.[1] In the United States, 48 per cent of the members of the total workforce, representing some sixty-nine million Americans, are over age forty.[2] In a society that is still in the grips of a youth obsession – baby boomers trying fruitlessly to hang on to their youthful bodies and skills – it is easy to figure out that the way organizations communicate with the employees will have to change. The situation in health care is especially acute, since the workforce through much of the last century was typically younger than in many other industries. Aging employees want information about different things than do younger employees, and healthcare managers have to provide that information in a way that avoids any sense of discrimination.

Clearly, the most important aging group that healthcare organizations need to communicate with is their current and potential patients and clients. Marketers know that the words we choose to communicate our messages are all-important in gaining the attention of the target. We can learn from them. To begin with, it seems that there is no one acceptable term to describe this group. *Senior citizen* is outdated and offensive to some. *Senior* is just as bad. *Old* is discriminatory. *Elderly* conjures up physical frailty. The term *mature* seems to bridge the gap between insulting and nondescriptive.

Once the labelling is out of the way, you will face other communication considerations. One important consideration for more mature audiences is the challenge of finding the right medium to reach them. Hospitals, health-service organizations, and long-term care facilities need to assess the usefulness of the materials they produce and the way these materials and messages are distributed to aging audiences. Here are some questions that may provide useful information in an evaluation of these materials.

1. Is the content applicable to an aging clientele?
2. Is the visual layout considerate to people with declining vision?
3. Is the material distributed in places that are likely to be frequented by aging clients? Or, perhaps, do you use direct mail (which is considered to be useful for this group)?
4. To what extent will Web-based communication vehicles be embraced by the mature public in your own sphere of influence?

Public Opinion

Another factor that alters communication from healthcare facilities is changing public opinion. Since your organization's image is a reflection of public opinion, how it changes is key to understanding how the external world thinks about you. Public opinion has always been mercurial, but changing demographics of the North American population are likely to magnify this fluctuation. Keeping communication current with public opinion is going to be a challenge for every manager in the healthcare industry.

Each passing day it seems, your audiences have more easily accessible information about health and health care. This proliferation of health-related information is a double-edged sword. On one hand, it does indeed serve to empower many consumers with enough information to somewhat balance that lopsided relationship that patients have traditionally had with healthcare providers. It truly makes them a part of the decision-making process about their own health status and healthcare decisions. On the other hand, however, a frighteningly large portion of the population has difficulty sifting through all of this available information. They have no frame of reference for determining what is truly useful to them and what is completely inaccurate.

Never before have we had so much genuinely valuable healthcare information so easily accessible. But, thanks in large part to online sources, never before have had we had access to so much spurious rubbish, either. Healthcare organizations have an increasingly important role to play as credible sources of information. Indeed, it may even be the case that they have a duty to assist consumers in this search for useful information. This might make the basis for a terrific community relations strategy.

Individual Attitudes toward Health Care

Another consequence of this increase in information is that attitudes toward healthcare decision making are changing. Even fifty years ago most decisions about health care were happily left to health professionals, mostly doctors. They knew best and paternalism was rampant. Now, however, public attitudes about who should be making these decisions and how they should be implemented are changing.

Communication implications for healthcare organizations are many. Are your employees knowledgeable about patients' rights? Do they have enough materials available to aid them in assisting patients? Are your employees aware of management's perspective on patient decision making? Do your patients/clients know their rights? Is your community familiar with your philosophy? These are just a few of the questions you have to be able to answer.

Fast-Forward Technology

Finally, communication technology changes almost daily and is likely to continue to change. Financial concerns notwithstanding, health-related organizations cannot afford to lag behind in communication technology. As a manager, it is important that you first recognize that access to the latest in communication technology is a strategic advantage. Second, you must be comfortable with the use of these technologies. When voicemail was first introduced into our workplaces, there were those who refused to embrace it or even learn how to use it. Then came electronic mail and few of us realized the extent to which it would revolutionize how we communicate. These two examples are only the beginning. Your own knowledge and comfort will enable you to ensure that others within your organization understand that these communication technologies are not only a nice addition to your organization's abilities, but may be crucial for their continued success.

These changes are already happening, and, in fact, may be better identified as trends. The bottom line is that the context of communication is continuing to change, and healthcare managers need to recognize these changes and adapt their strategies to them.

What Won't Change

Even amidst all this change, however, some very crucial issues will remain the same – the most important of which is the requirement for organizations of all kinds to recognize their social responsibility. Despite the fact that health-related organizations, by virtue of their very missions, consider their core work to be fulfilling a social responsibility, we need to examine the issue through a broader lens.

All organizations in society continue to exist only if they fulfil a societal need, only if they are serving a useful public interest. While at their core, health-related organizations seem to serve a vital public need, there must always be the public perception that the organization in question is doing so in a socially responsible way. In general, this implies that the organization fulfils its mission within the letter and spirit of the law at all times, has a code of ethics that guides its decision making, and that its activities reflect respect for human dignity and consideration for its larger community – in short, the organization is a good citizen. These actions are more powerful communication tools than any words that might come from your organization.

From time to time, it might be a useful exercise for health-related organizations to perform a social audit. This is a tool that you design to identify and assess your "social and environmental impacts, communicate internally and externally [your] performance, and make continual improvements in such areas as community and customer relations, employment practices, human rights issues, environmental responsibility, and ethical behavior."[3] This definition implies that communication is at the heart of a social audit. The results may help your organization to formulate directions for not only future communication priorities, but for operational priorities as well. Again, public perception of your organization's activities is at the heart of the matter.

Keeping Your Communication Strategic

Although the broader context of your communication activities and those of your organization continue to change and develop, there are some things that managers need to do to keep their communication strategic. Here are a few ideas.

1. *Ensure that you treat all audiences as special.* We have talked previously about the issue that one size definitely does not fit all. Careful consideration must be given to determining the informational needs, desires, and habits of a variety of constituencies for your organization. Indeed, your own communication practices should always consider this: in everything from composing e-mail messages to making public presentations.

2. *Enhance opportunities for two-way communication both internally and externally.* As attitudes about shared decision making and participation continue to change, it is more important than ever for you to consider how much feedback you invite and what you do with it. This needs to be true two-way communication, not lip service to asking for feedback and then ignoring it. Strive to enhance your communications with employees, clients, medical staff, board members, and the community at every opportunity to truly engage with them – not just listen, nod, and ignore. .

3. *Keep up with new advances in media technology.* This may require you to take a course. Even if you are at the highest level in your organization, don't rely on others to take up the slack here. As we have discussed all along, communication is a requirement of everyone, and you, as a manager, need to have more than a passing acquaintance with the new technologies. Right now: Do you know how to use Twitter? Do you use it strategically? Do you have a social media policy in place? Do you know how to search blogs online? These are some very simple media technology questions that no healthcare manager should answer "no" to at this point.

4. *Practise and hone your communication skills.* Your own personal skills – writing, presenting, giving media interviews – all need to be assessed and updated continually. Make use of your public relations staff if you have one available. Look for workshops and seminars. Attend communication sessions at health management conferences. Read.

5. *Keep an open mind to enhance creativity in healthcare communication encounters.* This is necessary on both a personal level and on

an organizational level. An old way of approaching a communication challenge may be just that – old. Always be open to new ideas
and strategies.

In summary, respect the power of communication. It has outcomes
that are both planned and unplanned, and you must be aware of these
at all times. You should never be caught off guard by any consequence
of your communications with anyone, at any level, in any situation.

Ethics and Communication

The power of communication is the very reason that ethical considerations are paramount. *Primum non nocere*: First, do no harm. Anyone
who has worked in the healthcare industry, even for a short time, is
familiar with the first commandment of ethics – to do good and to do
no harm. And communication can indeed be harmful if not approached
with a consideration of its ethical underpinnings.

Honesty

The primary ethical consideration in healthcare communication, as in
all other brands of public communication, is the responsibility to be
honest in all undertakings. Religious traditions throughout the world,
despite their wide differences, all exhort us to be honest. Indeed, integrity in organizational behaviour is crucial to maintaining positive relationships with all of your important constituencies. Honesty is one
crucial part of integrity, which implies doing the right thing even when
no one is watching.

Fairness

Fairness is also important in healthcare communication. Treating all
your audiences as if they are important ensures that your communication efforts reflect your respect for them. Fairness implies that all those
constituencies will be considered when planning a communication
effort and that you will deal with them honestly in all encounters.

Politeness

For the healthcare manager personally, behavioural guidelines can
enhance the ethical stance of your communication. It seems fitting that

we should end our discussion of how communication for healthcare managers goes beyond persuasion with a note about ordinary politeness. It is truly amazing what good manners, which by their very nature imply respect for others, can do in communication encounters. Can you answer "yes" to all of the following questions?

- Do you always say "thank you" to those who assist you even when it is part of their job?
- Do you always say "please"?
- Do you never reprimand a subordinate in front of others?
- Is your temper always well controlled?
- Is your language always appropriate and free of vulgarities?
- Do you completely avoid sexist remarks and/or ethnic slurs?
- Do you always refer to others with the degree of formality you expect for yourself?[4]

You need to be able to honestly answer "yes" to all of these as a basis for integrity and credibility in your communication efforts. Guidelines for your behaviour have the last word.

Rules of Behaviour for Healthcare Managers

- Focus on your own work and not on that of others unless you have specific responsibility for their work.
- Be conscientious and honest at all times. This will become a part of your reputation.
- Be cautious about self-disclosure. Employees and peers do not need to know everything about you.
- Give credit where credit is due. Ensure that those you supervise receive credit for their work rather than taking it for yourself.
- Take responsibility for your own actions. Don't pass the buck.
- Subscribe to a code of ordinary politeness.

It is impossible to manage without communicating. The notion that managers in healthcare organizations could begin their careers without formal instruction in communication – both personal and strategic – is beyond comprehension. What healthcare managers in the twenty-first century need to know, however, is that communication goes far *beyond persuasion*; and skilful communication is essential to successful achievement of your organization's mission.

Notes

Preface

1 William Choctaw, *Avoiding Medical Malpractice: A Physician's Guide to the Law* (New York: Springer Science and Business Media, 2008), 15.
2 Sharon Buchbinder and Jon Thompson, *Career Opportunities in Healthcare Management. Perspectives from the Field* (Sudbury, MA: Jones & Bartlett Publishers, 2010), 8.
3 Ibid., 126.
4 Jamie Haeuser and Paul Preston, "Medical Staff Collaboration: Communication Strategies That Get Results," *Healthcare Executive* 21, no. 4 (2006): 10.
5 Presented by the American College of Healthcare Executives, Chicago.
6 Jamie Haeuser and Paul Preston, "Communication Strategies for Getting the Results You Want," *Healthcare Executive* 20, no. 1 (2005): 20.

1. Communication: A Management Tool

1 Robert Katz, "Skills of an Effective Administrator," *Harvard Business Review* 52, no. 5 (September–October, 1974): 91.
2 David Conrad and Robert Newberry, "Identification and Instruction of Important Business Communication Skills for Graduate Business Education," *Journal of Education for Business* 87, no. 2 (2012): 118.
3 Patricia Parsons, *A Manager's Guide to P.R. Projects: A Practical Approach* (Mahwah, NJ: Lawrence Erlbaum, 2003).
4 Stephen Robbins and Mary Coulter, *Management*, 11th ed. (Scarborough, Ontario: Prentice Hall Canada, 2012).

5 Henry Mintzberg, *The Nature of Managerial Work* (New York: Harper and Row, 1973).
6 William Zinsser, *On Writing Well* (New York: Harper Collins, 2006), 17.
7 Frank Dance and Carl Larson, *The Functions of Human Communication* (New York: Hold, Rinehart, and Winston, 1976), appendix A.
8 Parsons, *A Manager's Guide to P.R. Projects.*
9 Robert R. Ulmer, Matthew W. Seeger, and Timothy L. Sellnow, "Post-crisis Communication and Renewal: Expanding the Parameters of Post-crisis Discourse," *Public Relations Review* 33, no. 2 (June 2007): 130–4. Communication & Mass Media Complete, EBSCOhost (accessed 13 September 2012), doi:10.1016/j.pubrev.2006.11.015.

2. The Strategic Communication Process

1 Alan Zuckerman, *Healthcare Strategic Planning: Approaches for the 21st Century*, 3rd ed. (Chicago: Health Administration Press, 2012), 15.
2 *New Illustrated Webster's Dictionary of the English Language* (New York: PMC Publishing Company, 1992), 742.
3 Ibid., 772.
4 "About Massachusetts General Hospital," http://www.massgeneral.org/about/overview.aspx (accessed 4 September 2012).
5 Hospital for Sick Children, http://www.sickkids.ca/aboutsickkids/who-we-are/vision-mission-values/index.html (accessed 4 September 2012).
6 St Jude Children's Hospital, http://www.stjude.org/mission (accessed 4 May 2011).
7 Griffin Hospital, http://www.griffinhealth.org/AboutUs.aspx (accessed 4 May 2011).
8 Shannex, http://shannex.com/vision-mission-and-core-values.html (accessed 4 September 2012).
9 American Nurses' Association, "About ANA," http://www.nursingworld.org/FunctionalMenuCategories/AboutANA.aspx (accessed 4 May 2011).

3. Interpersonal Skills

1 Patricia A. Wheeler, "The Importance of Interpersonal Skills," *Healthcare Executive* 20, no. 1 (2005): 44.
2 Over the years I have used and adapted these myths from a long-ago source that I have finally been able to locate on the Internet: Peter Griffiths, "Communication Fables Exploded," *Daily Herald*, 2 January 1988, http://www.lib.sk.ca/DH-Communication-Fables-Exploded (accessed 15 January 2013).

3 Attributed to William Cobbett, British journalist (1763–1835).
4 Shri Henkel, *Successful Meetings: How to Plan, Prepare and Execute Top-Notch Business Meetings* (Ocala, FL: Atlantic Publishing, 2007).

4. Put It in Writing

1 William Zinsser, *On Writing Well* (New York: Harper Collins, 2006), 17.
2 *New Illustrated Webster's Dictionary of the English Language* (New York: PMC Publishing Company, 1992), 957.
3 There are many editions of this book, the 50th anniversary edition of which was published in 2008.
4 William Strunk Jr and E.B. White, *The Elements of Style*, 3rd ed. (New York: MacMillan, 1979), 66.
5 Wilma Davidson, *Business Writing: What Works, What Won't* (New York: St Martin's Griffin, 2001), 6.
6 Gerald Alred, Walter Oliu, and Charles Brusaw, *The Professional Writer: A Guide for Advanced Technical Writing* (New York: St Martin's Press, 1991).
7 For a theoretical explanation of the psychological underpinnings of these varied approaches, see the work of American social psychologist Leon Festinger, who postulated the theory of cognitive dissonance, and Austrian psychologist Fritz Heider, whose balance theory was elaborated upon in his most famous work "The Psychology of Interpersonal Relations." This, along with a review of Aristotle's *pathos*, *ethos*, and *logos*, help us to understand the process of persuasion.
8 Zinsser, *On Writing Well*, 7.
9 For further information on e-mail etiquette, visit Laura Stack, "12 Tips for Better Email Etiquette," MS Office online, http://office.microsoft.com/en-us/outlook-help/12-tips-for-better-e-mail-etiquette-HA001205410.aspx (accessed 23 July 2013).

5. Presentations That Deliver

1 Jerry Seinfeld, *Public Speaking Quotes,* http://www.speech-time.com/public-speaking-quotes.html (accessed 17 May 2011).
2 Bert Decker, *You've Got to Be Believed to Be Heard* (New York: St Martin's Press, 1992).
3 Roger Ailes, *You Are the Message: Secrets of the Master Communicators* (Homewood, IL: Dow-Jones Irwin, 1988), 9.
4 Dale Carnegie, *The Quick and Easy Way to Effective Speaking* (New York: Pocket Books, 1962), 17.

5 Scott Berkun, *Confessions of a Public Speaker* (Sebastopol, CA: O'Reilly Media, 2010), 18.

6 "Choose a Pattern of Organization," Allyn & Bacon Public Speaking Web site, http://wps.ablongman.com/ab_public_speaking_2/24/6223/1593275.cw/index.html (accessed 27 September 2011).

7 Catherine Graham Bell, *Managing Your Image Potential*, 2nd ed. (Kingston, Ontario: Prime Impressions, 2001).

8 Doug Malouf, *How to Create and Deliver a Dynamic Presentation* (Brookvale, New South Wales: Simon and Schuster Australia, 1993).

9 Ibid.

10 Clella Jaffe, *Public Speaking: Concepts and Skills for a Diverse Society*, 6th ed. (Boston: Wadsworth, 2010).

11 Richard Zeoli, *The 7 Principles of Public Speaking: Proven Methods from a PR Professional* (New York: Skyhorse Publishing, 2008), 170.

12 Obviously, PowerPoint™ is the most ubiquitous of the lot; there are new platforms available every day it seems. Try the free, online presentation framework *Prezi* for a more-up-to-date, interactive approach to slides (http://prezi.com/) or *SlideRocket* for a place to create and share your slide presentations (http://www.sliderocket.com).

13 For further information on available online software for presentations see "Forget PowerPoint: 13 Online Presentation Apps," http://mashable.com/2008/02/16/forget-powerpoint-online-presentations/.

14 *New Illustrated Webster's Dictionary of the English Language* (New York: PMC Publishing Company, 1992), 926.

15 Ibid., 280.

16 If you are unfamiliar with the various uses of wikis, we'll discuss these more in the next chapter, and you can visit Common Craft's video *Wikis in Plain English* at http://www.commoncraft.com/video/wikis.

6. Fundamentals of Social Media

1 Andrew Keen, *The Cult of the Amateur: How Blogs, MySpace, YouTube and the Rest of Today's User-Generated Media Are Destroying Our Economy, Our Culture and Our Values* (New York: Doubleday, 2007).

2 This definition is the one I developed some years ago for the Canadian Public Relations Society's *CPRS Policy Statement Communications in Social Media* (http://www.cprs.ca/files/CPRSPolicy-SocialMedia.pdf) and captures what social media consists of and the most important characteristic of social media: participation.

3 Manhattan Research, "75% of U.S. Physicians Own Some form of Apple Device ...," http://manhattanresearch.com/News-and-Events/Press-Releases/physician-iphone-ipad-adoption (accessed 6 July 2011).

4 Manhattan Research, "New Study Shows Internet Directing Consumers' Choice of Health Services and Products," http://manhattanresearch.com/News-and-Events/Press-Releases/consumers-internet-health-services (accessed 6 November 2012).

5 Pew Research Center, "The Online Healthcare Revolution," http://www.pewinternet.org/Reports/2000/The-Online-Health-Care-Revolution.aspx (accessed 6 July 2011).

6 Pew Research Center, "Federal Health Privacy Regulation Does Not Cover Most Internet Media Searches, Services, or Purchases," http://www.pewinternet.org/Press-Releases/2001/Federal-health-privacy-regulation-does-not-cover-most-Internet-medical-searches-services-o.aspx (accessed 6 July 2011).

7 The Change Foundation, "Using Social Media to Improve Healthcare Quality: A Guide to Current Practice and future Promise," http://www.changefoundation.ca/docs/socialmediatoolkit.pdf (accessed 6 July 2011).

8 Jessica Squazzo, "Best Practices for Applying Social Media in Healthcare," *Healthcare Executive* (May/June 2010), http://www.ache.org/abt_ache/MJ10_F3reprint.pdf (accessed 27 September 2012).

9 Traditionally the term *mash-up* is used to refer to a Web page that uses data, presentation methods, or functionality from a number of different sources resulting in a new approach. The term now means any muddling together of a number of different elements resulting in a new creation.

10 Children's Hospital of Los Angeles, "Share Your Story – Use and Access," http://www.chla.org/site/?c=ipINKTOAJsG&b=5245675 (accessed 6 July 2011).

11 Social Media Governance, http://socialmediagovernance.com/policies.php (accessesd 23 July 2013).

7. Communicating In-house

1 Mary Welch, "Appropriateness and Acceptability: Employee Perspectives of Internal Communication," *Public Relations Review* 38, no. 2 (2012): 246–54.

2 Rodney Gray and Larry Robertson, "Effective Internal Communication Starts at the Top," *Communication World* 22, no. 4 (July/August, 2005): 26.

3 Cited in John Finney, "A World of Difference," *Communication World* 23, no. 4 (July/August, 2006): 34.

4 *New Illustrated Webster's Dictionary of the English Language* (New York: PMC Publishing Company, 1992), 241.

5 Robert Taormina, "Organizational Socialization: The Missing Link between Employee Needs and Organizational Culture," *Journal of Managerial Psychology* 24, no. 7 (2009): 651.

6 Johnson & Johnson, *Credo,* http://www.jnj.com/wps/wcm/connect/ c7933f004f5563df9e22be1bb31559c7/our-credo.pdf?MOD=AJPERES (accessed 19 May 2011).

7 "Reputation Management: I Believe," (1998), http://www.prcentral.com/ rmmj97j&j.htm (accessed 5 May 2000).

8 The Kennedy Group, "Culture vs. Climate," http://thekennedygroup. com/_pdfs/culture_vs_climate.pdf (accessed 6 November 2012).

9 Peggy Nuttal, *Nursing as a Career* (London: B.T. Botsford, 1960).

10 Kenneth Cohn, "Collaborative Culture," http://healthcarecollaboration. com/collaborative-culture/ (accessed 6 November 2012).

11 Kenneth Cohn, "A Practicing Surgeon Dissects Issues in Physician-Hospital Relations," *Journal of Healthcare Communication* 54, no. 1 (2009): 6.

12 Ibid., 5–6.

13 Victoria George and Alan Dundes, "The GOMER: A Figure of American Hospital Folk Speech," *Journal of American Folklore* 91, no. 359 (1978): 568–81.

14 Originally published in 1979, *The House of God* was re-released in paperback and electronic format in 2010.

15 Jitendra M. Mishra, "Managing the Grapevine," http://www.analytictech. com/mb119/grapevine-article.htm (accessed 6 November 2012).

16 Diana Morris, "Less is More: The Case Against Open Communication," *Journal of Employee Communication Management* (March–April, 1999): 10.

8. Communicating Strategically with Your Board

1 Cyril Houle, *Governing Boards: Their Nature and Nurture* (San Francisco: Jossey-Bass, 1997), 1.

2 Ed Sim, "Communicating with Your Board," *Beyond VC* (2007), http:// www.beyondvc.com/2007/01/communicating_w.html (accessed 30 May 2011).

9. Working with PR and Corporate Communications

1 Scott Cutlip, Allen Center, and Glen Broom, *Effective Public Relations*, 8th ed. (Upper Saddle River, NJ: Prentice Hall, 2000), 530.

2 Ibid.
3 Dennis Wilcox, Phillip Ault, and Warren Agee, *Public Relations: Strategies and Tactics*, 5th ed. (New York: Addison Wesley Longman, 1998), 396. See also the updated 10th edition by Dennis Wilcox and Glen Cameron (Boston: Allyn & Bacon, 2011).

10. Creating Community Relationships

1 Peggy Simcic Brønn, "Why Aren't We Measuring Relationships?" *Communication World* 25, no. 1 (January 2008): 32–4.
2 Warren Burkett, *News Reporting: Science, Medicine and High Technology* (Ames: The Iowa State University Press, 1986), 105.
3 Stephen Banks, *Multicultural Public Relations: A Social-Interpretive Approach*, 2nd ed. (Thousand Oaks, CA: Sage, 2000), 61.
4 By definition, social marketing refers to the application of the strategies, tools, and tactics of marketing to the promotion of social, often health-related, issues for the purposes of changing behaviour. This is distinct from cause-related marketing in which a for-profit entity takes on a social cause with the ultimate goal of promoting products. For example, when a brewery implements a drinking and driving strategy, they are doing cause-related marketing.

11. Media Relations Process and Practices

1 Warren Burkett, *News Reporting: Science, Medicine and High Technology* (Ames: The Iowa State University Press, 1986), 100.
2 Connie Kristiansen, "The British Press's Coverage of Health: An Antagonistic Force," *Media and Information Australia* 47 (1988): 56–60.
3 Maria E Len-Rios et al., "Health News Agenda Building: Journalists' Perceptions of the Role of Public Relations," *Journalism and Mass Communication Quarterly* 86, no. 2 (2009): 315–31.
4 Ed Shiller, *The Canadian Guide to Managing the Media* (Scarborough, Ontario: Prentice Hall Canada, 1994), 78–9.

12. Communication in a Crisis

1 *New Illustrated Webster's Dictionary* (New York: PMC Publishing Company, 1992), 235.
2 Timothy Coombs, *Ongoing Crisis Communication: Planning, Managing and Responding*, 3rd ed. (Thousand Oaks, CA: Sage, 2011), 2.

3 Albert Tortorella,"Crisis Communication; If it Had a Precedent, It Wouldn't Be a Crisis," *Communication World* (June 1989), http://www.highbeam.com/doc/1G1-7388486.html (accessed 29 November 2011).
4 SARS (severe acute respiratory syndrome) is a virulently infectious respiratory disease that circulated worldwide in 2002–3. Caused by a corona virus, it originated in China.
5 Craig DuHamel, "Dealing with SARS: Toronto Hospital Learned to Survive Beyond the Crisis Communication Plan," *Communication World* 20, no. 5 (August–September 2003): 30. For another perspective on this case see Craig DuHamel, "Using Lessons from SARS in Tackling Swine Flu: Looking Inward to Develop a Crisis Communication Model," *Journal of Communication in Healthcare* 2, no. 4 (November 2009): 395–410.

13. A View to the Future

1 "Canada: Median Age of Workforce Goes Over 40 for First Time in 2006," *Aging Workforce News,* 7 March 2008, http://www.agingworkforcenews.com/2008/03/canada-median-age-of-workforce-goes.html (accessed 11 July 2011).
2 IMEC, "The Aging Workforce in America," http://www.imec.org/imec.nsf/All/Aging_Workforce?OpenDocument (accessed 11 July 2011).
3 Arthur Parsons and Patricia Parsons, *Health Care Ethics* (Toronto: Wall & Emerson, 1995), 146.
4 Adapted from ibid.

Bibliography

Ailes, Roger. *You Are the Message: Secrets of the Master Communicators.* Homewood, IL: Dow-Jones Irwin, 1988.

Allyn & Bacon Public Speaking Web site. *Choose a Pattern of Organization.* http://wps.ablongman.com/ab_public_speaking_2/24/6223/1593275.cw/index.html. Accessed 27 September 2012.

Alred, Gerald, Walter Oliu, and Charles Brusaw. *The Professional Writer: A Guide for Advanced Technical Writing.* New York: St Martin's Press, 1991.

American Nurses' Association. *About ANA.* http://www.nursingworld.org/FunctionalMenuCategories/AboutANA.aspx. Accessed 4 May 2011.

Banks, Stephen. *Multicultural Public Relations: A Social-Interpretive Approach.* 2nd ed. Thousand Oaks, CA: Sage, 2000.

Bell, Catherine Graham. *Managing Your Image Potential.* 2nd ed. Kingston, Ontario: Prime Impressions, 2001.

Berkun, Scott. *Confessions of a Public Speaker.* Sebastopol, CA: O'Reilly Media, 2010.

Brønn, Peggy Simcic. "Why Aren't We Measuring Relationships?" *Communication World* 25, no. 1 (January 2008): 32–4.

Buchbinder, Sharon, and Jon Thompson. *Career Opportunities in Healthcare Management: Perspectives from the Field.* Sudbury, MA: Jones & Bartlett Publishers, 2010.

Burkett, Warren. *News Reporting; Science, Medicine and High Technology.* Ames: The Iowa State University Press, 1986.

"Canada: Median Age of Workforce Goes Over 40 for First Time in 2006." *Aging Workforce News,* 7 March 2008. http://www.agingworkforcenews.com/2008/03/canada-median-age-of-workforce-goes.html. Accessed 11 July 2011.

Canadian Public Relations Society. "CPRS Policy Statement Communications in Social Media." http://www.cprs.ca/files/CPRSPolicy-SocialMedia.pdf. Accesssed 29 July 2013

Carnegie, Dale. *The Quick and Easy Way to Effective Speaking.* New York: Pocket Books, 1962.

Change Foundation, The. "Using Social Media to Improve Healthcare Quality: A Guide to Current Practice and future Promise." http://www. changefoundation.ca/library/using-social-media-to-improve-healthcare-quality-part-1/. Accessed 6 July 2011.

Children's Hospital of Los Angeles. "Share Your Story – Use and Access." http://www.chla.org/site/?c=ipINKTOAJsG&b=5245675. Accessed 6 July 2011.

Choctaw, William. *Avoiding Medical Malpractice: A Physician's Guide to the Law.* New York: Springer Science and Business Media, 2008.

Cohn, Kenneth. "Collaborative Culture." http://healthcarecollaboration.com/collaborative-culture/. Accessed 6 November 2012.

Cohn, Kenneth. "A Practicing Surgeon Dissects Issues in Physician-Hospital Relations." *Journal of Healthcare Communication* 54, no. 1 (2009): 6–10.

Conrad, David, and Robert Newberry. "Identification and Instruction of Important Business Communication Skills for Graduate Business Education." *Journal of Education for Business* 87, no. 2 (2012): 112–20. doi: 10.1080/08832323.2011.576280.Coombs, Timothy. *Ongoing Crisis Communication: Planning, Managing and Responding.* 3rd ed. Thousand Oaks, CA: Sage, 2011.

Cutlip, Scott, Allen Center, and Broom Glen. *Effective Public Relations.* 8th ed. Upper Saddle River, NJ: Prentice Hall, 2000.

Dance, Frank, and Carl Larson. *The Functions of Human Communication.* New York: Holt, Rinehart, and Winston, 1976.

Davidson, Wilma. *Business Writing: What Works, What Won't.* New York: St Martin's Griffin, 2001.

Decker, Bert. *You've Got to Be Believed to Be Heard.* New York: St Martin's Press, 1992.

DuHamel, Craig. "Dealing with SARS: Toronto Hospital Learned to Survive Beyond the Crisis Communication Plan." *Communication World* 20, no. 5 (August–September 2003): 26–30, 48.

Finney, John. "A World of Difference." *Communication World* 23, no. 4 (July/August, 2006): 34–7.

George, Victoria, and Alan Dundes. "The GOMER: A Figure of American Hospital Folk Speech." *Journal of American Folklore* 91, no. 359 (1978): 568–81.

Gray, Rodney, and Robertson, Larry. "Effective Internal Communication Starts at the Top." *Communication World* 22, no. 4 (July/August, 2005): 26–8.

Griffin Hospital. "Mission Statement." http://www.griffinhealth.org/ About-Us.aspx. Accessed 4 May 2011.Griffiths, Peter. "Communication Fables Exploded." *Daily Herald,* 2 January 1988. http://www.lib.sk.ca/ DH-Communication-Fables-Exploded. Accessed 15 January 2013.

Haeuser, Jamie, and Paul Preston. "Communication Strategies for Getting the Results You Want." *Healthcare Executive* 20, no. 1 (2005): 16–20.

Haeuser, Jamie, and Paul Preston. "Medical Staff Collaboration: Communication Strategies the Get Results." *Healthcare Executive* 21, no. 4 (2006): 8–14.

Henkel, Shri. *Successful Meetings: How to Plan, Prepare and Execute Top-Notch Business Meetings.* Ocala, FL: Atlantic Publishing, 2007.

Hospital for Sick Children. "Vision, Mission, Values." http://www.sickkids.ca/ aboutsickkids/who-we-are/vision-mission-values/index.html. Accessed 4 September 2012.

Houle, Cyril. *Governing Boards: Their Nature and Nurture.* San Francisco: Jossey-Bass, 1997.

IMEC. "The Aging Workforce In America." http://www.imec.org/imec.nsf/All/ Aging_Workforce?OpenDocument. Accessed 11 July 2011.

Jaffe, Clella. *Public Speaking: Concepts and Skills for a Diverse Society.* 6th ed. Boston: Wadsworth, 2010.

Katz, Robert. "Skills of an Effective Administrator." *Harvard Business Review* 52, no. 5 (September–October, 1974): 90–102.

Keen, Andrew. *The Cult of the Amateur: How Blogs, MySpace, YouTube and the Rest of Today's User-Generated Media Are Destroying Our Economy, Our Culture and Our Values.* New York: Doubleday, 2007.

Kennedy Group, The. "Culture vs. Climate." http://thekennedygroup.com/_ pdfs/culture_vs_climate.pdf. Accessed 6 November 2012.

Kristiansen, Connie. "The British Press's Coverage of Health: An Antagonistic Force." *Media and Information Australia* 47 (1988): 56–60.

Len-Rios, Maria E. et al. "Journalists' Perceptions of the Role of Public Relations." *Journalism and Mass Communication Quarterly* 86, no. 2 (2009): 315–31. doi: 10.1177/107769900908600204.

Malouf, Doug. *How to Create and Deliver a Dynamic Presentation.* Brookvale, New South Wales: Simon and Schuster Australia, 1993.

Manhattan Research. "75% of U.S. Physicians Own Some form of Apple Device ..." http://manhattanresearch.com/News-and-Events/Press-Releases/physician-iphone-ipad-adoption. Accessed 6 July 2011.

Manhattan Research. "New Study Shows Internet Directing Consumers' Choice of Health Services and Products." http://manhattanresearch.com/

News-and-Events/Press-Releases/consumers-internet-health-services. Accessed 6 November 2012.

Massachusetts General Hospital. "Mission Statement." http://www. massgeneral.org/about/overview.aspx. Accessed 4 September 2012.

Mintzberg, Henry. *The Nature of Managerial Work*. New York: Harper and Row, 1973.

Mishra, Jitendra. "Managing the Grapevine." http://www.analytictech.com/ mb119/grapevine-article.htm. Accessed 6 November 2012.

Morris, Diana. "Less is More: The Case Against Open Communication." *Journal of Employee Communication Management*. Accessed from *Ragan's Employee Communication*. http://www.motivateandinspire.com/ME2/ Audiences/dirmod.asp?sid=04BF7B8C765E455DA06A7B6781ED0847&nm= Link+Grabber&type=Publishing&mod=Publications%3A%3AArticle&mid= 8F3A7027421841978F18BE895F87F791&tier=4&id=5B168B402F884999AD961 93A7EF4FF73&AudID=C9AF08199DF9479CA33AD783205471FA. Accessed 29 November 2012.

New Illustrated Webster's Dictionary of the English Language. New York: PMC Publishing Company, 1992.

Nuttal, Peggy. *Nursing as a Career*. London: B.T. Botsford, 1960.

Parsons, Arthur, and Patricia Parsons. *Health Care Ethics*. Toronto: Wall & Emerson, 1995.

Parsons, Patricia. *A Manager's Guide to P.R. Projects: A Practical Approach*. Mahwah, NJ: Lawrence Erlbaum, 2003.

Pew Research Center. "The Online Healthcare Revolution." http://www. pewinternet.org/Reports/2000/The-Online-Health-Care-Revolution.aspx. Accessed 6 July 2011.

Pew Research Center. "Federal Health Privacy Regulation Does Not Cover Most Internet Media Searches, Services, or Purchases." http://www. pewinternet.org/Press-Releases/2001/Federal-health-privacy-regulation- does-not-cover-most-Internet-medical-searches-services-o.aspx. Accessed 7 July 2011.

Pew Research Center. "Study Shows That Internet Searches Are Affecting Users' Healthcare Decisions." http://www.pewinternet.org/Press- Releases/2000/Study-Shows-That-Internet-Searches-are-Affecting-Users- Healthcare-Decisions.aspx. Accessed 6 July 2011.

Robbins, Stephen, and Mary Coulter. *Management*. 11th ed. Scarborough, Ontario: Prentice Hall Canada, 2012.

Seinfeld, Jerry. *Public Speaking Quotes*. http://www.speech-time.com/public- speaking-quotes.html. Accessed 17 May 2011.

Shannex. "Mission and Core Values." http://shannex.com/vision-mission-and-core-values.html. Accessed 4 September 2012.

Shiller, Ed. *The Canadian Guide to Managing the Media*. Scarborough, Ontario: Prentice Hall Canada, 1994.

Sim, Ed. "Communicating with your Board." *Beyond VC*, 2007. http://www.beyondvc.com/2007/01/communicating_w.html. Accessed 30 May 2011.

Squazzo, Jessica. "Best Practices for Applying Social Media in Healthcare." *Healthcare Executive* (May/June, 2010). http://www.ache.org/abt_ache/MJ10_F3reprint.pdf. Accessed 27 September 2012.

St Jude Children's Hospital. "Mission Statement." https://www.stjude.org/stjude/v/index.jsp?vgnextoid=9dc4b8ca05604210VgnVCM1000001e0215ac RCRD&vgnextchannel=f67c1e3d40419210VgnVCM1000001e0215acRCRD. Accessed 4 May 2011.

Strunk, William, Jr, and E.B. White. *The Elements of Style*. 3rd ed. New York: MacMillan Publishing, 1979.

Taormina, Robert. "Organizational Socialization: The Missing Link Between Employee Needs and Organizational Culture." *Journal of Managerial Psychology* 24, no. 7 (2009): 650–76. doi: 10.1108/02683940910989039Tortorella, Albert. "Crisis Communication: If It had a Precedent, It Wouldn't Be a Crisis." *Communication World* (June 1989). http://www.highbeam.com/doc/1G1-7388486.html. Accessed 29 November 2011.

Ulmer, Robert R., Matthew W. Seeger, and Timothy L. Sellnow. "Post-crisis Communication and Renewal: Expanding the Parameters of Post-Crisis Discourse." *Public Relations Review* 33, no. 2 (June 2007): 130–4.

Welch, Mary. "Appropriateness and Acceptability: Employee Perspectives of Internal Communication." *Public Relations Review* 38, no. 2 (June 2012): 246–54. doi: 10.1016/j.pubrev.2011.12.017.

Wheeler, Patricia A. "The Importance of Interpersonal Skills." *Healthcare Executive* 20, no. 1 (2005): 44–5.

Wilcox, Dennis, Ault Phillip, and Warren Agee. *Public Relations: Strategies and Tactics*. 5th ed. New York: Addison Wesley Longman, 1998.

Zeoli, Richard. *The 7 Principles of Public Speaking: Proven Methods from a PR Professional*. New York: Skyhorse Publishing, 2008.

Zinsser, William. *On Writing Well*. 30th anniversary edition. New York: Harper Collins, 2006.

Zuckerman, Alan. *Healthcare Strategic Planning: Approaches for the 21st Century*. 3rd ed. Chicago: Health Administration Press, 2012.

Index

About the Author

Patricia J. Parsons

Patricia J. Parsons is currently Professor of Communication Studies and a past chairman of the Department of Public Relations at Mount Saint Vincent University, Halifax, Nova Scotia, Canada. Professor Parsons teaches communication ethics and strategic planning in the four-year Bachelor of Public Relations, the Master of Arts (Communication), and the Master of Public Relations programs. She was the founding coordinator of the Bachelor of Science (Science Communication) degree program at MSVU where she has developed the health communication coursework.

Her research and writing have focused primarily on healthcare communication issues and ethics in public communication practice.

She is the author of ten books and dozens of papers for the professional, academic, and lay press including *Ethics in Public Relations: A Guide to Best Practice* (Kogan Page, 2004, 2nd edition 2009), and *A Manager's Guide to PR Projects: A Practical Approach* (Taylor & Francis, 2003).

An associate editor of the *Journal of Professional Communication*, Professor Parsons is an accredited member of the Canadian Public Relations Society and was admitted into the CPRS College of Fellows in 2005.

Visit her online at
http://backstorywriting.wordpress.com
http://www.patriciajparsons.com
Twitter: @pparsons07